gardens with atmosphere

gardens with atmosphere

creating gardens with a sense of place

Arne Maynard

with Sue Seddon

conran
OCTOPUS

Dedicated to my godmother Helen Smith,
who opened my eyes to gardens

First published in 2001 by
Conran Octopus Limited
a part of Octopus Publishing Group
2–4 Heron Quays
London E14 4JP

www.conran-octopus.co.uk

Publishing Director: Lorraine Dickey
Senior Editor: Muna Reyal

Creative Director: Leslie Harrington
Designer: Lucy Holmes
Picture Researcher: Mel Watson

Production Director: Zoe Fawcett
Production Controller: Alex Wiltshire

British Library Cataloguing-in-Publication Data. A catalogue record for this book is available from the British Library.

ISBN 1 84091 158 1

Colour origination by Sang Choy International, Singapore

Printed in China

title page Dorset woodland sweeps right up to this contemporary wooden house creating a powerful atmosphere without the need of a formal garden.

right The backbone path cut through to Jonathan Keep's arresting totem sculpture draws the eye through the garden and creates a powerful contrast with the wild-flower meadow beneath the apple trees.

Contents

right A topiary sentinel marks the threshold between house and lane inviting the visitor through the gate and setting up the atmosphere of the house and garden that are to come.

page 8/9 A traditional pond and meadow strewn with ox-eye daisies is given a spark of contemporary energy by a spiralling plume of water. It breaks the thick carpet of duckweed to create a shining disk on the pond's surface.

introduction

A sense of place is the soul of the garden. It is the intangible and harmonious atmosphere that stems from a perfect balance between the house, garden, landscape, plants and, importantly, the dreams of the owner. The result is a garden that feels absolutely right in its setting. The quality of light, the sound of the wind, the texture of the plants and the smell of the earth, leaves and flowers all add to its unique atmosphere. And that sense of place seems to seep out of the soil and link the garden back to nature. It creates an atmosphere in which you can quietly relax and reflect, and where time seems to cease. Once inside, the outside world disappears and you are in a timeless and personal Eden.

One of the strongest elements in these rich layers of influence is our ability to sculpt and mould nature. A garden's sense of place is an autobiography of its custodians, and reflects their philosophy, tastes and passions. Successive gardeners leave their mark, and the footprint of who and what went before should be respected and reconnected to the present. When I came to my own garden in Lincolnshire the site had a very strong spiritual quality to which I stayed true, making sure that any changes enhanced its sense of tranquillity and peace.

To create a sense of place you need a treasure chest of influences for your imagination to play with, but that chest can take time to fill. My own goes back to when I was three years old, which is when I started to garden. I had a tiny plot where I grew vegetables and flowers. By the time I was 11, I was looking after the whole garden, although what I did to it now seems pretty scary. Luckily, my sensitivities developed the more I went to look at other gardens, and I came to realize that the gathering of information is one of the most important factors in gardening. My design philosophy is to reinterpret what I absorb to make unique gardens that are in harmony with their setting.

That means there are no rules to break, and the influences can come from all parts of life – mine include art, architecture and nature. The secret is to recognize the things you like, and to use them to create a special and magical atmosphere. Nostalgia is an important ingredient because gardens are places of memory and association. I like to evoke wonderful things that happened in the past. I may give them a new twist, but the challenge and excitement is in creating something that is rooted in tradition yet still contemporary.

A sense of place is more easily recognized than created. I always suggest that when people move house they live with their new garden for a while before they make changes. I usually allow a year to understand a garden and its setting, and that includes the surrounding landscape and architecture. And I really like to get to know the owners and their way of life so that I can inject something of that into the design.

A garden is never finished: there are always plans for the future and the fun is that you can go on. The sense of place keeps evolving and ripening as the garden matures. It is always positive and when you create a wonderful atmosphere most people find it mesmerizing. It touches our inner self, we recognize its beauty and it re-establishes our ties with nature, the wellspring of all that is good in gardens.

Arne Maynard

flat landscape

A flat landscape is powerful and dominant. The sky is huge and the vistas stretch to the horizon, almost unimpeded. There is a sense of openness, adventure and discovery tinged with an exciting uncertainty of what lies beyond the boundary of the garden.

It is a fragile landscape too. The North American prairies and the English Fens are so wide open that you can see for miles, but a building or a pylon in an inappropriate place really stands out. And light pollution can be especially intrusive in a flat landscape where lights at night can make you realize that you share your seemingly rural idyll with hundreds of people and an industrial plant.

Such a landscape is full of energy and can be invigorating, and reactions to it can be extreme. Some immediately want to be protected from it, while others relish the sense of freedom and do not want to be shut

in. There are various ways of preserving the sense of excitement and freedom while at the same time, rationing the feeling of vulnerability and exposure that such a huge landscape can bring.

In a garden in open countryside it is a good idea to create vertical structures, such as hedges or walls, which create a comforting, safe haven and a sense of scale in such a vast sea of land. They will also help give some shelter and shade from wind and sun, creating a place of warmth and calm that has excellent contrasts with the flat, open spaces outside the garden.

Openings in the structure, such as sculptured gaps in a hedge also let in the vast sky and space beyond the boundary and sustain the mood of excitement and surprise that gives the garden another dimension. And pergola posts, clumps of trees, pleached trees and small buildings and other such devices give points of interest and reference to the scale of the landscape.

Not everyone wants to be shut in. In the past, people who owned land wanted to look out at what was theirs, and sometimes created subtle boundaries such as ha-has so that they could survey the land beyond the garden boundary. This device can be applied to a small cottage garden today. In fact, it is sometimes better to open up such a garden to the landscape to give more sense of space. One device that works well is to make a link with the landscape by bringing plants from beyond the boundary into the garden – a knot garden filled with corn, poppies and cornflowers, or a low hedge of field maple and hawthorn. Details like this complement the starkness of the landscape.

left Echoed in the simplicity of the garden a vast landscape is brought effortlessly to the heart of the house through the transparency of the building.

top right Simple and effective: opening up the boundary to the landscape beyond can be as straight-forward as weaving the branches of a hedge into a circular frame.

bottom right In North America zig-zag fences of local wood make strong but see-through boundaries. They are an excellent way to create movement and interest in a vast landscape.

wooded landscape

left A path leads through a mesmerizing sea of bluebells. The horizontal blue carpet balances the vertical pillars of the woodland trees.

top Setting sculpture in woods can make a powerful link with the cultivated garden. Here, the sculptor Andy Goldsworthy's serpentine wall snakes through trees drawing us deeper into the woodland landscape.

bottom A stone gate pier makes a strong visual connection from the garden across the canopy of trees to the church beyond.

A wooded landscape is in complete contrast to open countryside. Here the mood is one of leaving the world behind. Tranquillity, secrecy and mystery mingle like the dappled light on the woodland floor. There is a sense of being alone and at one with nature, but the mood is not threatening, it is calm and introverted.

Different types of wood create different moods. Pine is beautiful, but can be dark, sinister and brooding. Strong horizontal lines of light-coloured planting in the garden, such as a beech hedge, and simple, rather minimalist structures create a feeling of openness and prevent the wood from overpowering the garden.

Where a deciduous wood meets the garden, you need a different approach. Draw people through the garden into the wood via paths and little gateways, or cut a gap in the hedge creating a link. Pulling the wild woodland planting into the garden – the turkscap lily (*Lilium martagon*), snowdrops, primroses or bluebells – helps to sustain the sense of place too. And if there is room, the boundary can be feathered out to meet the landscape by a graduated planting of the same woodland trees at the end of the garden.

If the wood beyond the garden boundary is part of the property, then the link between garden and wood can be delicately woven with paths that continue through the wood, and clearings for rustic chairs and tables or even a maze made of logs. Keeping the eye on horizontal interest takes it away from the relentless verticals of the trees. Nature does this with horizontal carpets of bluebells under woodland trees.

And sometimes there is a case for creating no garden, in the usual sense of the word, at all. There are situations where the wood is all, and can be allowed to come up to the windows of the house, bar a strip of clearing to allow in some light. Here, the sense of place, the stillness and quiet and the filtered light from the canopy of leaves is so strongly wrought by nature that interference is almost sacrilege.

mountains and hills

You can't compete with mountains. A garden that has them beyond its boundary should acknowledge their presence at almost every turn. Such spectacular scenery is emotionally charged, testing, dangerous and full of energy. The sense of place is powerful and challenging when the landscape is so definitely beyond our control.

Of course, the weather and the environment may limit what you can do, but a place to sit and view all this is essential. Some form of seating area can be made of local materials or decking. It is best placed on the edge of the garden so that nothing impedes the view or the sensation of being out there alone with the spectacular scenery.

A garden high up in the mountains does not need too much structure. It should blend with its surroundings by integrating plants and local materials: steps can be cut out of the rock, and plants, such as house leeks, that grow in the area should be planted in the garden. The whole effect should be quite rugged and the boundary left open to the scenery.

Lower down, the mountains may be distant, but you still need to think big to balance the view. Large paths leading to lush meadows, big stone terracing and features, such as bold sculptures, will enhance the mood and complement the grandeur of the scenery.

Hills feel safer than mountains and their mood is usually more stable. They can be tranquil, mysterious, and energizing. A glimpse of hills is guaranteed to fill you with hope and make you want to head for them.

If the hills can be seen from everywhere in the garden it can lessen the impact of the view. One way to heighten the effect is to create surprise vistas, and this can be done by planting a hedge that apparently shuts out the view. A gap or doorway in the hedge

top The delicate and informal planting at The Garden House, Devon, forms a sympathetic balance between the garden and the far-reaching hills beyond.

middle In Provence vernacular plants have been sculpted into powerful mounds to reflect the shape of the distant hills, creating harmony between the natural shape of the landscape and the cultivated order of the garden.

bottom A poetic device: poet and artist Ian Hamilton Finlay created these traditional stone walls with poetic words. They concentrate the mind and vision on the beauty of the upland landscape.

left Pyramids of beech mirror the architecture and link house and garden. In an urban environment they provide privacy, a green foil and wildlife shelter.

above Cityscapes can be beautiful, especially if viewed from a roof terrace. Here, simple planting allows the view its full power.

On the whole, we want to shut out what is beyond the boundary of the town garden. It depends, of course, on the nature of the townscape: a magnificent view of city skyscrapers, an ancient cathedral or church spire are views worth opening up, but an ugly urban building or industrial site are not. The most important way in which a townscape influences the town garden is the search for peace and privacy in the teeth of the frantic turmoil of today's towns and cities. We want somewhere that is a complete contrast to the traffic, noise and bustle. We want to shut all that out and create a personal green haven full of calm.

All gardens are about calm, whether they are of the urban, minimal, no-time-to-garden variety, or the country-garden-brought-to-the-town kind. Both have their place in bringing another dimension to the urban dweller's life. However, a town garden does not have to ignore what is beyond the boundary; it can work with it. It is quite possible to create a design for a green space with clear, crisp, minimal lines that reflect what is going on outside.

Small spaces, such as courtyards or roof terraces, often need a powerful feature such as a large urn, sculpture or topiarized tree to compete with the mayhem of architectural styles over the wall. A small courtyard can also look stunning with water pouring over a sheet of stainless steel or glass, especially if it is lit at night by fibre-optic lights. In fact, a table, chairs and two huge pots of box balls are all you need to create a powerful green space. Its simplicity holds its own against the complex urban jungle, but it is a space where you can relax with a glass of wine at the end of a hectic and gruelling day.

Many town gardens are extensions of the living space. They are often used as eating areas and a small courtyard transforms to a dining room very easily. Awnings are useful in town gardens as they preserve privacy. A simple canvas awning on poles need not be expensive, but it will define the eating area and screen you from the neighbours.

There are larger gardens in towns, and for the most part, they bring the country to town. There may be room for a rose garden, a lily pond, herbaceous borders and even beehives. The *rus in urbe* look is a direct reaction against the townscape beyond the boundaries. An alternative green utopia is a jungle-type garden where lush, thick planting, can perhaps include tall bamboos to shut out the urban surroundings and create absolute privacy. It can be quite magical with a profound sense of place.

Another outside influence on town gardens is light pollution from surrounding streets. It is difficult to overcome this but, if there is room, trees and strategically placed screening of some kind, such as ivy-clad trellis, help. Lighting the garden can detract from street lamps too. In contrast, enclosed courtyards may have some very dark areas, and limewashing the walls can bring light and colour into the garden where there is not much room for plants.

the plants

Plants play an important role in creating and sustaining the link between a garden and its surroundings; they may be indigenous or seen in other gardens. Indeed, in towns, this may be the only plant link to the locality. Discovering what grows in the wild or is grown locally is a great help as it shows which plants thrive in the local soil. Local plants strengthen the sense of place by tying the garden into the landscape.

Cultivated plants are not necessarily indigenous but over time gardeners have found that particular kinds thrive in certain places. In Cornwall, for example, crocosmias and fuchsias are grown everywhere. In a sense, they have become vernacular or social plants, passed from garden to garden by generations of gardeners, with a strong local sense of place and they can be used in a newly designed Cornish garden, though not necessarily in a traditional way.

Wild plants can also be incorporated into the planting plan, tying the garden into the landscape. Plants should be bought from specialist nurseries and never taken from the wild, which is illegal in Britain.

You can also use the planting pattern of the land-scape to create new and exciting schemes that still relate to the surrounding countryside. Plants from beyond the boundary can be used in a formal setting, such as corn or flax to infill a parterre, or cow parsley as an edge softener. These types of plantings mirror many different landscapes from rolling farmland to wooded hillsides and valleys. Using plants by integrating them in this subtle way links the formal to the informal, and the garden to the landscape.

Contrasts of plants work well too. The backdrop to a garden might be a beautiful beech wood. A strong, dark, sculptural yew hedge at the boundary will heighten the colour and delicate tracery of the beech, and act as a foil between the cultivated and the wild.

The portfolio of plants to use depends on the garden site. If it is set in verdant water meadows plant reeds and grasses, or an avenue of stump willows. Apple trees are evocative of the countryside so plant them in orchards or as an espaliered hedge. Hawthorn makes a good hedge too, whether at the boundary or as the tiny hedges of a parterre infilled with a soft planting of double buttercups. Wild geraniums and orchids, cow parsley, cowslips and sanguisorba planted at the edge of the garden will merge it with the land-scape. All these plants can be used in other areas of the garden too.

The hot hills of the Mediterranean and California have an abundance of wild plants that will thrive in gardens. Box, juniper, rosemary, lavender, myrtles and herbs are all worth growing. Some, such as box and lavender, can be clipped to echo sun-baked hillsides. In colder climates, heathers work well in moorland areas. Scale is important too and if, for example, a garden opens out to the wide expanse of a lake, then willows, alders and hornbeams will help to keep a balance between the garden and the vastness of the landscape.

top left Knowing that cow parsley and wild geranium are growing in your woodland-edge garden makes it feel at one with the landscape.

top right The light at the sea is so bright that gardens can take flowers in strong colours but grasses, hebes and stachys do well too.

bottom left Euphorbia, blue iris and clumps of low-growing hebes edge the path that climbs through a hill garden.

bottom right A countryside combination of apple trees underplanted with a profusion of white ox-eye daisies and pink wild baptisia.

house
and garden

introduction

A house and its garden should be at one with each other. The rapport between them is fundamental to a sense of place, and houses that jar with their surroundings rarely have the necessary sense of calm and harmony. The relationship between house and garden stems from the architecture, and to get the balance right I begin by looking at the architecture of the house because it dictates the style of the garden. I would rarely put cottagey plants such as roses and lavender with a contemporary house. However, this does not mean that an ancient building can never have a contemporary garden.

The interior of a house, and the lifestyle and tastes of the people who live in it, are also vital ingredients in the mix that influences the garden's design. The garden should work sensitively with the interior of the house: a pattern from the interior panelling can be reproduced in a knot garden, or if a medieval house has a simple white interior with Giacometti furniture and contemporary paintings and sculpture, then a simple garden that refers to the past, but also looks to the future would be appropriate. Whatever the style of the interior, the garden should reflect it.

We spend so much time inside looking towards the garden, either from the kitchen sink or preferably from a comfortable chair, that the view from the windows is a key to the design and planting. An important link between house and garden is made at the threshold and the links that connect them are extremely important. The planting plays a major role whether it is a porch festooned with clematis and honeysuckle, or contemporary pots of herbs at the kitchen door.

Man-made or carved by time from nature, the size, shape and setting of the garden plot and where the house sits influence the mood of the garden. Some plots are full of atmosphere, while others need plenty of help to create a comfortable marriage between the house and garden. The plot's aspect and climate play important roles too, dictating the type of plants that will grow and the mood of the garden, whether it is cool, green and wooded or sunny, dry and peppered with hot pinks and oranges. The entrances to the plot add to the atmosphere and should welcome the visitor. Elaborate wrought-iron gates, gilded and coloured, or a simple oak gate with ox-eye daisies clustered at the foot can give an idea of the garden to come, and heighten the anticipation.

Looking back at the house from the garden is also crucial to creating a harmonious whole and the garden should frame the house. Architectural details of the house can be used in the design of the garden. The windows of a period house may, for example, have a pattern that can be used to create the basic shape of a parterre, or a wall can be built of the same stone as the house. Unifying the whole so that the garden almost becomes another room of the house adds to its mood. Such connections create the harmony between house and garden, so vital to a sense of place.

page 26/27 The framework supporting a hornbeam hedge takes its inspiration from the glazing bars of the house, the Prieuré d'Orsan in France, creating a living window through which to see the garden.

right At Elsing Hall in Norfolk the wild and simple planting is in keeping with the romantic moated and half-timbered house.

medieval and elizabethan

Palaces had pleasure gardens, but most gardens of the medieval period were about survival; they were for growing food and medicinal herbs. In response to the lawlessness of the times, medieval houses had blocked views. Houses and gardens were fortified with walls, and almost always had an atmosphere of introspection. Today, some courtyard and cloistered gardens remain, but even the garden of a medieval cottage is mainly for recreation. Some have a vegetable garden, but most owners of medieval houses want a garden in which to relax and entertain.

Of course, the precise style of the garden depends on the tastes and lifestyle of the owner, but there are features of medieval gardens that can be incorporated into a design. Such elements make a strong link to the architecture of the house and enrich the sense of place. Structure and symmetry were the prime features of medieval gardens and they are qualities that we still like because they make us feel safe and comfortable. To create a link between house and garden I create enclosed spaces with simple knots and topiary, and plants supported by willow hoops in small, ordered raised beds, edged with low wattle fencing. Painted timber

arbours and palisades, turf seats, fountains, and poles surmounted with heraldic beasts and a turf maze add to the feel.

I also use some modern plants because the medieval plant palette was very limited and mostly consisted of herbs for healing, cooking, dying cloth and making perfume. These included herbs such as sweet cicely, rue, feverfew, hyssop and borage, and irises and gillyflowers (carnations) were also popular. Many features, however, can be given a contemporary twist. I might plant beds with herbs and plants of today such as monardas and echinaceas, and edge them with oak boards. Beds edged with boards painted blue and planted with acid green euphorbia and black tulips have a strong echo of a medieval garden, but an extremely contemporary feel.

Elizabethan gardens evolved from medieval ones, but since the need for fortification had gone, houses and gardens looked outward. Many were for pleasure and show, rather than food production. And the Renaissance gardens of Italy had a strong influence as people travelled more.

The Elizabethans made extremely good use of pattern; it appears in the panelling,

plasterwork and decoration of houses, and on clothes and textiles. Pattern is therefore highly appropriate when designing gardens for houses of the period.

Controlling nature is another Elizabethan theme that lends itself to garden design. The Elizabethans trained plants on frames, and generally manipulated nature, so it is worth creating pleached lime walks in a garden as they are redolent of the period, together with fountains and pools, walkways leading to knot gardens or an orchard with a central mount.

A perfect lawn is not an Elizabethan concept, and if I create a lawn around an Elizabethan house I fill it with violets, cowslips and daisies. I like to contrast man's formality with nature so I make wild flower meadows with paths cut through long grass set with topiary. On the same theme, formal gardens enclosed by picket fences close to the house contrast well with flowery meads beyond. The aim is not to create designs that are slavish recreations of Elizabethan design ideas but to capture the essence of the period.

far left, top Hatfield Old Palace was built in 1497 and the re-created knot garden is based on garden designs of the Tudor period.

far left, middle and bottom Patterns to design a knot garden can be taken from a half-timbered house, interior plasterwork, strapwork embroidery, or a fireplace by the great Elizabethan stone mason and architect Robert Smythson. Using pattern in this way forms a link between a house and garden.

above Within an enclosure of woven hazel branches this medieval garden is well matched with its ancient house at the Weald and Downland Museum, Sussex. The garden is planted with practical plants for medicinal and culinary use.

late 17th to 18th centuries

The gardens of the late seventeenth century were, like their Elizabethan predecessors, about pattern, but were more refined and on a bigger scale. The emphasis was on creating a sense of openness. Long vistas and axes, grand *allées* of pleached trees, wilderness gardens with statues and pavilions, and broad walks cut through long grass epitomize the period. Paths were important and set out in formal patterns. There were also huge parterres sparsely planted with a few specimen plants, such as tulips or fritillarias as these new and exotic plants were arriving in England from plant collectors all over the known world. The gardens that surround Ham House in Surrey, are a prime example.

Many gardens of the period were hardly on a domestic scale and were more like grand feats of engineering. Recreating them today is inappropriate and beyond most budgets, but when I design gardens for a William and Mary house there are elements that can be used. The formal parterres can be imitated on a smaller scale, and the passion for pattern and symmetry can be recreated as oval or lozenge-shaped beds, or crisp areas of grass set in lime chippings. Using low box hedging to create patterns also gives the right period feel, and if there is room, so does a wilderness garden, which might have a contemporary sculpture rather than draped classic figures that used to grace such gardens.

Country gardens of the Georgian period were quite different. The great landscape movement brought the surrounding park right up to the windows of the house. It may have looked simple but this Arcadia was sophisticated and playful, with grottos, hermitages and trophies from the Grand Tour incorporated into the garden. Exotic plants such as pineapples and oranges had whole buildings devoted to their care. The Georgians also loved to make collections of plants such as auriculas and hyacinths.

To create an appropriate garden for a Georgian house today, I would concentrate on the axes and vistas and create surprises which reflect the designs of the period. I prefer to take away all the inappropriate features, such as nineteenth-century flower beds, that have been added to the garden over the centuries. I might also reinterpret the idea of garden buildings, of which the Georgians were very fond. However, instead of a temple dedicated to Diana, I might make

a boat house, picnic lodge or a castellated cow shed. Simple buildings, probably made of wood, can be fun and organic.

Across the Atlantic, eighteenth-century colonial houses in North America clung to the William and Mary garden styles for a little longer. These were always toned-down versions, slightly more rustic and naive in feel, which suited the wooden buildings well. The gardens of these charming houses often had potager-type areas for growing vegetables and herbs. To keep the spirit of such gardens, I might design cottage garden hedges with fruit trees and topiary and a long path to the door, bordered by flowers with ordered beds of lavender and vegetables on either side.

above At Ham House, Richmond, Surrey, the Cherry Garden evokes the purity of late seventeenth-century design with its clipped and manicured box, simplicity of planting and broad gravelled walks.

far left Early seventeenth-century garden design was taken to North America by the early settlers. Colonial North American gardens retained the style and it survived for centuries longer than it did in England.

victorian and edwardian

Victorian domestic architecture looked back to medieval gothic and the Tudor and Jacobean styles. This produced the quirky nineteenth-century architectural hybrid known as 'Jacobethan'. The gardens that set off these styles were fired by a torrent of plants brought from around the world. Growing techniques improved, and the Victorians had the manpower and technology to sustain elaborate gardens of colossal parterres full of bedding plants.

To retain atmosphere and sympathy with Victorian architecture, a garden of the twenty-first century might have several sections such as a rose garden and herb and vegetable gardens. Topiary was also a Victorian favourite and can be softened with misty plantings such as bronze fennel with love-in-the-mist. I repeat the more refined elements of Victorian planting schemes like campanulas with roses, and jazz up the planting in some areas with pots of bright red salvias or petunias.

If the house is gothic revival in style, then I go back to heraldic medieval ideas, seeking inspiration from the topiary gardens at Levens Hall in Cumbria. Recreating the mysterious, romantic and spooky atmospheres as found in some Scottish gardens is fine. Mazes also have a very Victorian feel. However, I might not make a hedge maze, which is expensive but cut one in the long grass of a flower meadow.

Gardens of the Edwardian period were more leisure oriented and gardening became popular, even with those who employed gardeners to do the work. The aristocracy rolled up its sleeves and began to prune, plant and clip. Edwardian gardens featured big herbaceous borders, wide grassy walks, rose gardens, herb gardens, tennis courts and bowling greens. Houses had big windows that looked out onto the garden. The English country house look, like that at Heale House in Wiltshire, came into being during the Edwardian period. Edwin Lutyens and Gertrude Jekyll, that exceptional teaming of design, architecture and planting, began the movement and their influence is still strong today.

Many Edwardian gardens still have good backbone and sense of place. However, some replanting is an option. Today, we have better and more disease-resistant varieties of Edwardian favourites, such as Michaelmas daisies, and they are well worth planting.

right The design of this house respects and embraces an existing tree resulting in a wonderful contrast between old and new, nature and man-made.

far right The integration between house and garden is extremely well achieved. Water laps against the terrace and tumbling plants drape the building like a contemporary Hanging Garden of Babylon.

20th century and contemporary

In the first half of the twentieth century most garden design was stuck in the Edwardian period. Two world wars had brought the luxury of innovation to a standstill through the need to produce food and the lack of manpower and funding. Things began to move forward in the 1960s, but mostly in institutions, businesses and public spaces rather than domestic gardens. Then, gradually, the ideas of twentieth-century architects such as Arne Jacobson, Frank Lloyd Wright and Le Corbusier filtered through and began to influence garden design.

The new ideas, based on purity of design and minimalist planting, were very structured. The emphasis was on dominant, hard straight lines in which the planting was secondary to the landscaping. Concrete was used to make wide paths, and huge planters were installed containing shrubs such as *Fatsia japonica* and *Viburnum tinus*, and bedding plants such as busy Lizzies. There were few flowers and front gardens often had no boundaries between them.

During the 1960s, the Danish architect Arne Jacobson designed the buildings and gardens of St Catherine's College, Oxford. This green, cubist space is an inspiration for the sort of gardens I create for houses of the 1950s and 1960s. It has simple planting within blockish hedges that form sculptural shapes. I prefer to use stone rather than concrete, and I sometimes include a simple water feature, which goes well with the uncluttered shapes of landscaping and planting.

The contemporary garden is an extension of the house, and comes into its own as an outside room in an urban situation, although contemporary gardens in a country setting work extremely well too. Our knowledge of what is beyond the city boundary and linking the clear architectural lines of buildings with nature – the bluebells beneath the silver birch trees – are inspirations for this type of garden. Contemporary gardens can have an extremely strong sense of place, particularly when they create an oasis of calm in a teeming city life. The design of contemporary gardens highlights contrasts between materials, such as stainless steel and glass, and between materials and plants. It is also about simplicity, and that great design maxim, 'Less is more' applies to the planting as well as the hard landscaping of the backbone.

Quality is also a key to success. The architectural lines of the backbone – walls, paths, levels – and so on, should be of the best possible quality. A wall of beautiful stone, impeccably cut and topped by a lip of stainless steel over which water pours, can fit into the smallest garden. Together with one well-chosen plant, it may be all that is necessary to create a haven where the mind and body can relax.

The plant palette for these gardens is simple: single colours and varieties work well with strong architectural lines. Both the planting and architecture should be confident and of the same style so that there is an equilibrium, with neither dominating. Because so few plants are used they need to be chosen and placed with as much care as a single dot of colour on a contemporary painting. Plants can be stage managed for maximum impact; the planting is absolutely minimal – one olive tree against a wall is effective – but consequently extremely important.

Plants can be used in an architectural way, so in an urban garden I might make a mown cube parterre with blocks of long grass, bounded by copper beech or hawthorn. Using grass brings the echo of a wild flower meadow into places where it is unexpected. The plants are used to add architectural form, and planting is done in wedges and blocks so that the plants are actually used like sculpture or building materials.

In the countryside this contemporary feel is followed through by linking the landscape with the garden, keeping nature, ecology and environment to the fore. Gardens are not gardens in the conventional sense of the word. They can have a very natural and open feel by allowing what is beyond the boundary, whether open countryside, a wood, or an olive grove, to come right up to the walls of the house. Contemporary sculpture set in natural spaces such as woods, meadows or orchards works well in this context.

It is also possible to keep the open natural feel, while delineating the boundary, either round the whole garden or the part closest to the house. This can be done by building a wall, rather like a stage flat, behind one focal tree, a *Quercus ilex* perhaps. By limewashing the wall in a strong colour, the boundary is clearly defined but does not shut out the landscape. The tree is seen silhouetted against a vibrant wall that suggests a division between the inner and outer garden.

You can give a contemporary twist to an olive grove or an apple orchard by clipping trees that border a pathway into drums. It is manipulating nature in the much same way that eighteenth-century parkland and seventeenth-century topiary did. In contemporary settings, the plants are the antiques and contrast with the modern materials of the buildings. This contrast is what makes contemporary gardens so exciting and full of energy.

Land sculpture, in which the land is literally moulded into shapes, is another way to give a garden a contemporary ambience. My land sculptures draw on inspirations from the past as they have the imprint of Elizabethan

mounts and medieval turf mazes. For a 1960s house in Cornwall I created a minimalist garden with a simple planting of lime green lady's mantle and orange flowers with platforms of field plant hedges. The garden leads to a field that has a beautiful view of a bay.

The design of the field takes its inspiration from beyond the boundary. A sinuous path is cut deeply into the field, reflecting the deep Cornish lanes. Intermittently, curved banks with dry-stone walls run beside the top of the path echoing the dry-stone walls of the landscape. There are views through the gaps in these walls so that you can look through the wild flowers at eye level as you walk along the path. The path leads to a large spiral mount with water on one side. The whole scheme uses only native plants and local materials. It is maintenance free, apart from mowing the path, and ecological because the meadows are planted only with Cornish wild flowers.

right The bold, structured planting of clipped domes of lavender and santolina contrast well with the twisted trunks of the ancient olive trees. Both are set off to perfection by the powerful orange wall.

interiors

While the exterior of a house has an obvious influence on the design of a garden, the interior has a less immediately obvious, though equally important role to play. The interior holds a huge amount of information about the style, tastes, and interests of the people who live there. How people decorate their homes and the possessions with which they surround themselves are clues to their lifestyle and character, and important influences on the design and spirit of the garden.

Any interior will provide information and objects that may inspire a design in the garden. There may, for example, be a marvellous painting and if the colours are wonderful, it may be possible to pick them up in the planting scheme and draw the house, contents and owner's personality together in the garden. Or the geometric shapes in a painting or a sculpture can be used to form the basic pattern of a grass parterre, or a series of clipped hedge platforms.

Travel is another influence. People often have fond memories of eating outside in warm places and this can inspire dining areas in the garden. Plants, too, are evocative, and lavenders, *Magnolia grandiflora*, and potagers full of vegetables are redolent of holidays.

An interior, however, can be in complete contrast to the outside of the house. An Elizabethan or Georgian house may be minimalist inside with white walls, uncluttered spaces and contemporary furniture, paintings and sculpture. This contrast should be reflected in the garden, and the garden should suit the lifestyle of the house owners. All interiors are individual, but there are certain broad styles that quite often have very little to do with the architecture of the house.

The English country rectory look is one that dates hardly at all. It is the epitome of the country house, with bowls of flowers everywhere, rosebuds on the bedroom walls and chintz loose covers on the ample, comfortable sofas. The look is a mixture of many periods with classic oil paintings, timeless furniture and hardly anything contemporary in sight. The whole house has an air of being well designed and organized.

Gardens that match this style are quintessentially English. They are usually traditional and sometimes have a good backbone with brick paths, flagstone terraces, ponds, steps and walls. Hedges often divide the garden into rooms and there will be a herb garden, rose garden, vegetable garden, orchard and herbaceous borders.

The planting is ordered, and even when plants spill out over lawns and paths it is because they have been permitted to do so. The owners of such gardens are often good plantspeople. Such gardens are beautiful and timeless. The sense of place is strong and often requires little more than a few improvements to the backbone, on which to hang planting schemes.

The bohemian artistic interior is not out to create a 'look'. It is an eclectic collection of beloved artefacts including pottery, paintings, Staffordshire figures, postcards, fine china with mixed cups and saucers, books everywhere, marvellous old furniture, including shabby sofas of faded elegance, ethnic throws and layers of clutter. Nothing is tidy, vacuumed or dusted. The gardens are similar, often without much structure, full of beautiful things, but the atmosphere is wonderful. It is like stepping into a lost world of old apple trees with roses climbing through them, underplanted with pink tulips. There are ancient plant-swathed arches of metal and wood, and longish grass full of daisies where fallen apples attract blackbirds and butterflies. The border plants tumble on to grass and paths, and sculptures peer from the foliage. In this casual and

romantic Eden, owners and nature garden together. You do not tidy this sort of garden, but allow plants to grow between paving and cow parsley along the paths. The garden of Charleston Farmhouse, Sussex, is a good example.

A quite different style is often associated with medieval and Tudor homes. Big, blockish, dark oak furniture with linenfold panelling and tapestries and large oil paintings on the walls add to a

above and right The classic English country interior goes hand-in-hand with a garden of well-organized rooms: spacious lawns, rose gardens and herbaceous borders of delphiniums, campanulas, hollyhocks and hemerocallis. Such atmospheric gardens are often punctuated by topiary and surrounded by traditional hedges of yew and beech.

simple, bold look of muted colours. The associated garden has the same sort of feel with few flowers, big hedges, topiary, knot gardens, parterres, and mazes. Inspiration for its sense of place comes from the past and rejects manicured lawns, creating areas of long grass and flowery meadows with paths cut through and fat topiary. Oak picket fences, pleached trees, and courtyards with borders of hellebores create a harmony with the interior of the house.

The colonial look was originally rather minimal because settlers in the New World had so few possessions. The refined fruitwood chairs, plain linens, soft paintwork and naive designs began as basic emulations of their homeland.

Growing food was the prime purpose of the original colonial gardens, and when I design a garden in keeping I like a productive but ornamental mix of flowers, vegetables and herbs. I start from the position of the settlers who had no fancy materials, so I use local materials. I might make a picket fence of oak or ash branches and paint it with earth pigment. I create knot gardens, but may fill them with strawberries and rhubarb. Fruit trees, lavender and roses continue the style.

There are two contemporary looks. One has bright colours, fabrics with bold designs, steel, glass and stone or wooden floors. The other has a single palette with pale linen, natural woods, stone and neutral colours. Both have minimal furniture and the interiors are bold, architectural and functional.

The garden needs to match the styles. It is not about creating many garden rooms, but about creating

top and far right The rich interior of dark oak panelling and Delft plates (far right) could easily inspire a garden like the one at Beckley Park, Oxfordshire (top). The bold planting of box hedges and topiaried yew are in perfect scale and harmony with the Jacobean house.

bottom, left and right The free-spirited design of this simple interior needs a garden of similar style such as the relaxed and natural planting of cow parsley, foxgloves, and roses surrounding this idyllic plant-swathed house.

space. Contrasting materials and complementary colours are important, and the scale of the plants must match the architecture. Urban houses suit these looks well.

In one of my projects the black slate floor of the interior continues outside to the terrace and the garden steps. The garden is bounded by pleached copper beech trees underplanted with yew. Grass and a black cobbled path leading to a black slate fountain ensure that the living area and garden are in harmony.

above and right Full of freshness and energy, the wonderful New England interior (above) needs a garden that equals its simplicity and strength. The colonial garden (right) has an uncomplicated yet powerful backbone of box hedging with a single planting of orange hemerocallis in the foreground. It would make an ideal marriage with the New England interior.

plot

above When he uprooted
the native plants to build his
New Zealand house the artist
and architect Hundertwasser
replaced them on the roof
creating a house in absolute
harmony with its setting and plot.

Once architecture and style of
interior have been established it is
time to look at the plot. There are
two basic types: one is man-made
and usually urban, the other is
carved out of nature, an evolution
of the countryside and history. Both
are influenced by the surroundings,
and their sense of place comes
partly from their setting.

Man-made plots are usually
regular in shape, a row of small
Victorian houses in a village, or a
new estate in the suburbs often

have rectangular plots to fit into
their surroundings. As towns
encroach on the countryside,
larger plots of old houses are often
swallowed up, sold off in sections
as building plots and the remaining
garden left a more regular shape.
Urban plots are very different in
feel from a cottage garden whose
irregular shape has been carved
out of a field over time, perhaps
in order to grow vegetables. And
country gardens of ancient houses,
such as a moated plot, moulded by

antiquity and the landscape, often have a very strong sense of place.

Sometimes the atmosphere is endemic to the plot. It may be the way that the plot sits among hills, or the way a stream runs through it; the harmony of the separate elements creates the sense of place. This harmony can be fragile, so the plot needs sensitive treatment. The marriage between the position of the house, the plot and the surroundings must be comfortable. I once tackled an extremely flat garden that felt at odds with its rolling landscape. The plot and its atmosphere were transformed by gently undulating the lawn to match the countryside.

The position of the house in the plot plays a key role. Many Queen Anne and Georgian houses open straight on to the street. The approach does not reveal much about the house, its owners, or the garden. If the house has a large back garden it will have a magical, secret element of surprise, which you do not get if you travel through a front garden first. It is like entering a more private and personal space. However, a house set back in the plot, with a long front garden has a different atmosphere in which anticipation about the character of the garden

and its owners builds as you approach the front door.

When the house sits in the middle of a plot it is surrounded by an oasis of garden. This creates a mood that melds with the landscape, often giving it a peaceful and protected feel. Very steep plots that rise from the back of the house do not usually work well because the house can seem oppressed and claustrophobic and the garden very exposed. If, on the other hand, the house sits on the crown of a hill the atmosphere is often open, courageous and bold.

The size of the plot can contribute to its atmosphere too. Courtyard gardens can have a marvellous sense of place. Within them we are shut away in tranquillity, walled in an enclosing embrace that stems from primeval feelings of safety, protection and peace. Moorish courtyards in Spain still have this element, heightened because these havens of greenery and fountains often open from unpromising, claustrophobic alleys.

Large plots sometimes have room for a kitchen garden away from the house, which gives them a feeling of retreat and peace and a sense of being at one with nature. No matter what the size of plot, the bottom of a garden almost

always has an intense sense of place because it is furthest away from the rest of daily life.

Dividing the plot can also enhance the atmosphere. Some ancient plots are already divided by a lane or stream, but most plots need to be artificially divided. Simple screening in a small garden heightens the sense that there is something further to explore as do walls, hedges, or other devices in larger plots. These subdivisions add to the atmosphere of a garden by setting up expectation, secrecy and surprises.

Plots are also influenced by their aspect and climate. A garden that faces due south has a warm, colourful, musky, herby sense of place. It is buoyant and uplifting in mood and very different from a north-facing plot that will be cooler, greener and calming. Even in Britain, quite exotic plants grow where it is mild or the Gulf Stream has an influence: palms thrive on the west coast of Scotland, and ginger lilies and fuchsias grow happily in Cornwall. Where the climate is colder the sense of place is different: where trees are bent into Tolkeinesque shapes by the wind, the mood can be magical, eerie and mysterious because it is ruled by nature and not gardeners.

links

To create a good ambience and maximize the sense of place, a house and garden need to be linked strongly together. A house and garden that ignore each other can never have the powerful atmosphere that comes through integration. Links are made from the inside of a house looking out towards the garden, from the garden looking back at the house and at the threshold where you step from the house into the garden. How these links are arranged has a huge impact on the atmosphere of a house and garden.

From inside the house there is a pull that takes the eye out into the garden and beyond and this link depends on the axes through the house into the garden. For example, it is sometimes possible to step into the hall of a house and look straight through into the garden. An axis like that makes a very strong link between house and garden.

The most-used rooms in the house, such as the sitting room, should have good axes to the garden, especially the places where we sit to read or view the garden on a winter's day. Where the garden comes close to the house it is a good idea to create a beautiful formal garden so that there is

always something attractive to look at and to tempt the occupants out of doors on a good winter's day. Grow early-flowering plants in it such as witch hazel, hellebores, winter-flowering iris and sweet scented daphne. Spring bulbs also draw people out of doors, especially if there is a permanent seat near the kitchen door.

The kitchen is usually the most important room, being the hub of the house, and it needs an axis via windows and doors that takes the eye into the garden and beyond to the landscape. It also brings the garden back into the kitchen. This all-important axis can be improved by adding a door and creating a terrace with a place to eat in a sunny spot. If the kitchen cannot be changed, it may be possible to create a door to the garden in another room. Sometimes it is simply a matter of placing furniture differently so that there is a better axis to the garden.

Axes are like energy lines from the house to the garden and they help entice people to explore. They can be used to take the eye far out into the garden – to lengthen it, to make it more visually exciting, or lead the eye to a focal point. Sometimes, it may be better to block the view, especially in town

gardens. By planting a screen of plants, the way in which the eye travels around the garden can be manipulated and the accent put on a different route or focal point.

Stepping out into a garden should be a magical moment as it is laden with a sense of freedom, expectation and pleasure. The threshold is vital in building up the atmosphere of a garden. Planting should include layers of delicate tracery through which to glimpse the garden. It needs to be matched to the house with sensitivity and character and the plants should soften and set up the threshold so that you step through a wonderful porch of scrambling honeysuckle and roses, or see winter jasmine dripping past the windows.

Colour and scent are also powerful links. When you open the door fragrant plants such as summer jasmine and daphne fill the threshold with evocative perfume. Strong colours, such as cyclamen, in beds against the house help to anchor the house to the ground and give vibrant views from the windows. To make the link stronger, threshold plants can repeat colours from the interior.

Marking the threshold of house and garden increases the atmosphere and defines the

The area close to the house has long been used as an outdoor room. Eating outside is now a way of life and paved areas, loggias, arbours or canvas awnings make beautiful protected areas in which to enjoy a drink or a meal al fresco. Conservatories, verandas, decks and balconies are also excellent ways of making the link.

What is seen when looking back at the house from the garden is equally important. Terraced houses should sit easily in their setting. Large detached houses should have enough breathing space to create a transition between house and garden and should not sit on a skinny apron but stand as if on a pediment. A terrace or a platform of box hedge are dramatic ways of setting the house up and giving it importance, while plants in scale with the house will enhance its proportions when viewed from the garden.

far left A riotous vine creates a wonderfully soft transition between architecture and cultivation and makes a delightful link between house and garden.

left Rose-covered pergolas are always popular. This one provides a shady awning that protects the house and links it to various parts of the garden.

entrances

Gates are places of arrival and departure and carry all the accompanying emotions. Because it is the first thing you see when you arrive at the boundary of a property, a gate should always be welcoming and give a taste of what is to come. Grand wrought-iron and gilded gates flanked by ornate brick piers topped with pineapples or finials will not signal a tumble-down cottage, although a gap in a hedge or a rusty iron gate entwined with wild flowers may.

Seen from a road or lane, a gateway marks the way into a property and the route you need to make to get to the heart of the garden and the house. It is possible to read a lot into a gate and gateway. The degree of formality or informality, whether it is the main or side entrance, workmanship and design, materials and state of repair and the surrounding planting all play their part in helping create the character and mood of the garden.

Gates can have a very potent atmosphere. A pierced gate sets up a buzz of anticipation because parts of the garden can be seen through it, whereas a solid gate creates a surprise. The solid oak door that leads into the garden at my house in Lincolnshire heightens the effect of stepping from an open meadow into the magical surprise of a walled herbaceous garden. What a gate is set in also plays a part in this drama. A solid door is best set in a wall; a pierced gate really needs a hedge. The sense of arrival at both is extremely powerful and both clearly state 'This is my private space', but the pierced gate in the hedge creates a more casual approach while the solid door in the wall has an air of secrecy.

The atmosphere at the point of entry is also changed by the material, style and proportions of the gate. On approach, a garden may seem rather sterile and cold with little sense of intimacy, but the ambience of the approach can be changed by substituting a wide gate for a narrow one and putting rustic poles draped with clematis above. The plants around a gate are extremely important too. The planting can spill out in front of the gate in a relaxed and almost frivolous manner or tumble over an arched gateway. Scented plants such as roses and honeysuckle make a particularly beautiful and atmospheric entrance.

Gates set in the inward curve of a semi-circular wall (a device that Lutyens often used) form an embracing arm that draws the visitor in, and makes a gentle delivery into the garden. If the curve is outward it almost throws the visitor in and the approach is much faster. In contemporary gardens the entrance may not be framed in hedges or walls, but marked by a change of materials – a path may change from stone to grass or a textured entrance path may have different plants in it, for example, using thyme at the entrance to a herb garden.

Entrances may be welcoming, but they are also territorial and mark each individual's haven. Beyond the actual gate there is a zoning of degrees of privacy, and at each entry point they become more and more private and sacred. In large estates the visitor enters through a carriage gate and then possibly a line of trees arriving at a human-scale entrance, and then to the private heart of the garden. It is the same effect as arriving at a front gate beyond which is a route that, depending on its scale, has different speeds of delivery: a narrow winding path is relaxed with no sense of hurry; a wide, straight path is faster.

right A well-worn but welcoming doorway can evoke thoughts of the succession of past gardeners who have nurtured the secret garden behind it.

Within the garden there can be many other entrances. They set up a visual directory to the rest of the plot and are the catalyst for all the routes that you take through it: gaps in hedges, steps to another part of the garden set up surprises and reveal the unexpected. Sometimes there may be a partial view of another part of the garden glimpsed through a hedge, a gap in the wall, or a tracery of planting that can create a feeling of anticipation and suspense. Such garden entrances set up the change of environment and mark the end of one place and the beginning of something new, such as moving from a planting of bright hot colours into a cool green space.

The sound of a gate also gives an evocation of a place – the latch clicks, the gate clunks, the door creaks on its hinges. You may not know it, but the sound of a gate as it closes behind you as you enter a garden heightens your expectation. When you leave the feeling must be just as good. The click of the gate is a punctuation to the travels through the garden and the emotions it has created. And as you walk away you want to think, 'Ah, that was lovely...'.

top left The formality of these railings and the portico set up an expectation of the interior of the house and its garden.

top right The way in through a simple iron gate in the hedge is marked dramatically by large-scale topiary.

right An enticing driveway guarded by ancient lime trees draws visitors through parkland to the house and garden.

foundation blocks

introduction

When you step into a garden for the first time there are existing elements in place. They are the foundation blocks with which you work. In an established garden they may include walls, buildings, paths, steps, flower beds, an old orchard, or a beautiful tree. The garden of a new house will have foundation blocks too, like a view to the hills, some trees, perhaps even a stream or pond. Some will be right and some will be wrong and need changing.

Working on the foundation blocks involves deciding what to keep or enhance, and what to get rid of to establish a design and a sense of place for a particular garden. Everything that follows – the backbone of the design and the planting scheme – hangs on the foundation blocks. It is not a case of slash and burn to clear everything away, but a subtle and patient process. Patience is the key and, especially with an established garden, it is worth waiting a year and taking many photographs to record what grows where and when.

One late autumn, I designed a parterre for a garden. In the spring, when we were about to begin work, I visited the garden for a final check and discovered that the plot designated for the parterre was carpeted with wild orchids, a rare and marvellous discovery. The parterre was immediately assigned to a different part of the garden, leaving the orchids to flourish in peace and give that part of the garden its unique atmosphere.

Whether you restore the garden with historical accuracy or allow it to evolve is one of the great debates when dealing with the foundation blocks. The best result is usually a combination of the two, but judging what to keep and restore and what to create anew is the essence of creating a unique and right atmosphere – a sense of place. There may, for example, be some old apple trees. They may be well past their productive prime, but the ambience they give to the garden could not be reproduced with new trees. The gnarled trees have a wonderful nostalgic sense of place, and although they may be old, they are still a beautiful shape. Before you grub them up ask yourself what mood you want in the garden and balance that against a crop of apples from new trees.

On the whole, it is much too easy to destroy the very elements that give a garden a certain atmosphere. Try to keep in mind why you bought your house and garden – what were the elements that attracted you in the first place? A garden may be overgrown, but beneath the jungle it may have excellent foundation blocks that can become the basis for new planting design. Look around and observe, there is usually a practical solution to a problem. Go gently, the garden may have taken years to evolve, and it is best to respect the foundation blocks and build on them for the future.

page 56/57 An old laundry cistern beneath the boughs of a quince tree in an ancient garden in Provence has become a dipping pool in which to bathe in the open.

right A playful spiral of flint transforms old brick paving and brings atmosphere and art to a shady corner of this Dorset garden.

making an assessment

To make the selection process easier, the foundation blocks can generally be divided into two groups: elements that give the garden vertical lines, including buildings, walls and trees, and horizontals, such as paths, lawns, and terraces. Conserving the best of these will help to retain the garden's history and, like the patina on fine antique furniture, add to the richness of its ambience.

However, existing features do not have to be preserved in aspic and many can be improved and enhanced. Walls may have been recapped at some point and no longer match the antiquity of the house, but they can be sensitively restored to match, giving a subtle but significant change. Out-buildings are sometimes of hideous and unsympathetic materials such as breeze blocks, but if the building has good proportions and is in the right place it is worth keeping. Breeze blocks can be disguised with weather boarding, and once a well-proportioned window is in and the roof peg-tiled, an unpromising building can be transformed into a loggia for summer evening dining.

Hedges are often very over-grown in established gardens, but rather than take them out assess whether, with some radical cutting, they will be right for the garden. They may provide essential shelter and shade, or define a specific area. If a hedge has outgrown its original form and scale it can often be cut back to shape. If it has become extremely straggly and dead in parts, but is in the right place, it may be right to take it out and replace it. Hedges can also be opened up by cutting gaps to views beyond. Sometimes, though, hedging is simply of unsuitable plants that may be too oppressive and dark. Replanting with a different type of hedge transforms the foundation block and gives a much lighter, upbeat mood.

Trees make an important contribution to the foundation blocks as they give a sense of continuity and add vital vertical lines to the form of the garden. However, they can often be improved. A tree that was planted 50 years earlier may now obscure a view. It may simply be a case of removing the lower branches to open up the view again.

Trees sometimes have to be removed in the extremely important process of simplifying axes and vistas. A coppice wood at the boundary may be very beautiful, but may need opening up to brighten its claustrophobic atmosphere. The bold step of cutting a swathe to a seat, or a view of a church spire beyond, can improve the aspect immeasurably.

Some trees are features in their own right, but the beauty of their form is often obscured by an underplanting of shrubs. Clearing them can make a radical difference and restore the trees' contribution to the garden's atmosphere. Trees that are planted extremely close to a house can cause all sorts of problems and may have to be removed, but trees that stand guard over a house can also be magical. Again, it is a question of weighing up the benefits to create the right atmosphere.

Keeping certain foundation blocks can sometimes mean giving a part of the garden a different use. In one of my projects, espaliered fruit trees were so ancient it was no longer possible to walk along the path beneath them. But in age the the trees had gained a certain beauty that added to the garden's mood. In fact, their part of the garden was so steeped in atmosphere that removing them was not an option, so the path was rerouted and the original path was planted with bluebells, snowdrops and hellebores to add to the magical sense of place.

top Rusting outbuildings need not be demolished; they can be restored and given a new function.

middle If possible, old greenhouses should be restored as they bring great atmosphere to a garden.

bottom At Cranborne Manor, Dorset, an old yew hedge has been cut back, reshaped and rejuvenated.

right A coat of the right colour paint can transform old buildings and blend them into the newly made garden.

left Where water once flowed, erigeron now pours: a venerable garden feature, such as this ancient fountain, can be the starting point for a new design for a garden.

above An old damson tree acts as an identifier of the garden's past and can be included in the foundation blocks of a new design.

When assessing the foundation blocks of a garden, simplification is often the key to regeneration. A lawn can be transformed if fussy little shrubs are removed and it is restored to a perfect horizontal swathe of green. Whether lawns are kept and at what size often depends on how the garden is to be used, especially if children need somewhere to play. However, it is worth remembering that lawns make an excellent link between different areas and can unify a whole garden, so do not be too keen to get rid of them.

Besides lawns and levels, paths and terraces form the major horizontal features in a garden. Paths are often neglected, but if they are made of good materials such as old bricks or York stone they can be restored and, if necessary, rerouted. Old paths often add greatly to the mood of a garden, especially if they are weathered with moss and lichen and have plants, such as *Alchemilla mollis*, growing in the cracks.

A terrace can be equally important. You sometimes come across a glorious old house with a terrace of concrete slabs. In an extreme case like this the slabs have to be replaced with a more suitable material. A terrace may simply in the wrong place on the windy, sunless side of the house and need to be resited, using the original materials. This can occasionally mean creating another doorway from the house on to the terrace, but the benefits can be huge, giving the house a warm, sheltered terrace where you can eat breakfast or dine by candlelight.

Taking over a new garden may mean evaluating the plants. You may, for example, want more space to grow things and that can mean taking out some of the existing plants. But look at what you already have very carefully before you decide to remove things. Make sure that the lichen-encrusted viburnum you are planning to remove is not adding to the overall mood of the garden. A garden where everything is new, and nothing has weathered does not, generally speaking, have such a depth of atmosphere as a garden with a sense of age.

Existing plants can, however, be adapted and given a new twist. An old knot garden, or a parterre infilled with the rose 'Superstar' can look very dated. Take out the roses by all means, but the existing box hedge can have great character, especially if it has grown a little wavy. So clip and repair it and look at new ways to fill in the spaces that

left These box hedges were once infilled with roses, which have been taken out and replaced with platforms of yew with clipped central domes. They give a completely new look within the old foundation blocks.

right Working with what you have is important. These strong straight lines of lavender have been planted to echo the strength of the existing pool and balustrade and link them to the gate piers of the former entrance.

form the patterns between the ribbons of hedge. Try a less formal plant such as wild strawberries or scented tobacco plants.

Keeping a garden's sense of place means conserving some plants within it. What is already there may give you a wonderful planting and a colour scheme for the garden. Watching the existing plants through the seasons will give you an idea of what grows well and flourishes, and what seeds freely. These plants add character and individuality to the garden.

Borders can be rejuvenated by dividing congested clumps of herbaceous plants and taking cuttings of shrubs, which can be potted up and put back into the new structure of the garden. There may be unsuitable plants though, or those that are not your favourites, but before you dig them up, observe and photograph the border over a year. What comes up may have cross-pollenated and self-seeded and you may have some gems of plants, such as a tulip with a particular stripe, that is exclusive to you and your garden.

Many plants have actually been lost because, as fashions change, plants are ripped out and tossed on the compost heap. Among them are some Victorian varieties of primula, and several different kinds of rose and rosemary. So check what is growing in your garden before before you discard it.

It is important that we conserve our plant heritage, and taking care of what we have is vital. There is a gentle tradition of caring for plants that is reflected in a garden and conserving plants, especially old plants, is exactly what helps to give a garden a sense of place and time.

As you set about assessing the foundation blocks you have inherited, think boldly and create foundations for the future. This may include conserving some things from the past, such as a piece of old woodland. If some of the plants in your plot are past pride of place, think about regenerating them elsewhere in the garden so that you create new foundation blocks for gardeners of the future.

backbones

introduction

The backbone is the floor plan of the garden and it is the most vital element in garden design. It is like a skeleton and is the basic structure on which everything else, including the planting, is hung. A garden without a backbone is an amorphous and incoherent place. It lacks that special quality of form which, even in a small garden, effortlessly draws you through and leads you to vistas and surprises.

The backbone of a garden establishes the axes and vistas; the circulation or routes through the garden; the subdivisions or garden 'rooms'; the vertical walls or hedges, buildings, features and centrepieces; and the horizontals of lawns and cross axes. It also sets up the scale of the garden. A garden without a backbone, however simple, will always struggle to achieve the atmosphere that imbues it with a sense of place.

The structure of the backbone should connect the design and the soil. It should also anchor the garden in its setting so that it sits comfortably, and is perfectly at ease in the surrounding landscape. The house, garden and what is beyond the boundary should be drawn together by the backbone, giving a satisfying unity and framing the house and the views from the windows. The backbone takes the eye out from the house, whizzes it through the garden to the landscape beyond, or brings the landscape into the garden.

One particularly important function of the backbone is to create a structure that looks good in winter. When the backbone is right it gives the garden strength, form and purpose when most plants have died back, so that there is always something attractive to look at through the coldest and most bleak months, and something that will be glorious in the summer too. A simple knot garden seen from the house will look as beautiful dusted with frost as it does infilled with billowing flowers in high summer.

A garden's backbone can be formal or informal. My gardens usually have a symmetrical form. I think people relate to formality in gardens and buildings because there is great symmetry in nature. We quite like a formal backbone in the garden because it makes us feel that we can tame nature and imprint the plot with our identity. Of course, you can clothe the backbone, or dress it down to something more relaxed if necessary, and it can be disguised or made more dominant if that is what the garden and its setting need.

Different kinds of backbone can create different moods even within the same garden. For example, you might have a long axis or vista with walls on either side. The walls will create a very different feeling and atmosphere from two hedges. Both walls and hedges are architectural in feel, but the hedges will give a much calmer sense of place than the walls because they are soft, green, and more transparent, so you can glimpse what is on the other side. The walls create a much more severe and formal walk. They have a physical feeling of protection and permanence.

A successful backbone gives a structure that will stand the test of time and get better as it matures. A good backbone is timeless. The great Italian gardens of the Renaissance have such excellent backbones that many have lasted for centuries as have some old English gardens, such as Blickling Hall in Norfolk, where the great backbone of yew hedges has stood for 300 years. The backbone need not always be traditional. You can have a backbone that creates a contemporary feel, and although what is placed within it can change with fashion as new plants and colours come to the fore, a strong backbone will remain and hold the garden together.

page 66/67 A perfect example of how grass does not have to be flat. This turf maze is moulded out of the land creating a very strong link to the spirituality of the past, yet at the same time it makes a strong backbone that connects it to the landscape.

above and left The same garden seen in winter and summer. A really good backbone is extremely important as it carries the garden through the winter by giving it form and interest. This garden looks beautiful in winter and even better in summer.

axes, vistas and subdivisions

Axes are the signposts in the garden. They highlight different directions and routes and help to create the way the garden and its atmospheres are perceived. An axis is the strong line that you can walk and look along. It is the line from which the vistas stem and on which the garden's subdivisions are made. It can be thought of as the energy line that flows through the garden.

Axes link the house to the garden. They often begin at points where you step into the garden and they are the visual stimuli you see via a window or doorway that tempt you outside and then pull you through the garden. Large gardens may have more than one axis and can run down the garden and across it. Wherever they run they are the dominant backbone and lead the eye around the garden. From the main axes run sub-axes and together they set up the circulation, or routes, through the garden.

A smaller suburban garden may have only one axis. However, you can play tricks with the perspective of the axis: if the axis takes the form of a path the same width all the way down, the garden will appear long and thin, but if the path is widened towards the end the garden will appear wider too.

A vista is the view through the garden. It may take the eye beyond the boundary to a church tower, or a view of hills. The axis ends, but the vista continues and can change the mood of the garden.

Axes are usually for formal gardens where backbone is being created. They do not have to be straight and may not be necessary if the garden is casual and informal.

Once the axes are in place, the subdivisions can be made. They are the key to injecting different moods and atmospheres into the garden. A big, open garden can be seen at a glance but it has little in the way of excitement or sense of discovery or hidden areas. Subdivisions, or garden 'rooms' provide the interest.

In planning a garden with a sense of place it is essential to decide on the number, function and proportions of subdivisions for the plot. The best way to do this is to make a wish list. It can be as varied as the personality of the garden's owner: one might want water, an orchard, a vegetable garden, and a 'lunch lawn' under apple trees.

The subdivisions may be hedged in the same way, but the planting can make each part feel quite different. For example, an area surrounded with dark green yew and planted with a scheme of

green ferns, soft blues, yellows and whites has a feminine, cool, tranquil feel. The identical plot with eight geometrical topiarized trees and a fountain in the middle would be masculine, architectural, bold and strong.

In terms of backbone the mood of subdivisions is created by the height, width, texture and materials of the dividers. A brick-walled garden gives a different mood from a hedge, and a low hedge has a different feel from a tall hedge with an arch in it. Types of hedges vary the mood too: a hedge of hawthorn and field maple is much more relaxed in atmosphere than a neatly clipped yew. If you want to dress down the whole garden keep the dividers as natural as possible.

In fact, the divisions need not be vertical. A change of level as little as two steps up or down makes a good division between two areas, as does switching from a grass path to stone. It depends on the sense of enclosure, the size of the garden or a wonderful view that has to be kept open. Above all, look at as many gardens as possible: there is always something to learn.

above At Lytes Cary Manor, Somerset, the main axis is framed by topiary yews that lead the eye through the gate to the focal dovecote and then on to the vista of lime trees beyond.

far left, top Here, the backbone of sculptural hedges draws you in and invites you to explore further. The enticement to enter the subdivision is heightened by the round hole cut in the hedge and the red tropaeolum.

far left, bottom The coloured walls create a subdivision in this garden. They prevent the eye from travelling too far and pull it back to the asymmetrical focal point of the tree.

circulation, structures and focal points

The circulation through the garden is the device that keeps interest alive, inviting exploration. It entices you on, and in large gardens leads to changes in atmosphere and environment. Good circulation is stimulating and should make it clear which way you turn next. In fact, the axes, vistas and general circulation are extremely closely linked and should flow easily, guiding and enticing the eye to other parts of the garden, or to the landscape beyond.

Although the circulation must flow, there are points where the eye can be stopped to give breathing space and add to the anticipation and excitement of what comes next. These punctuation points are part of the backbone and say, 'Don't look too far, we don't want you to see everything at one go, the garden has some surprises for you.' Such points might be dividing hedges or walls, but they can also be structures such as pavilions, or eye-catchers like fountains. They may be readily visible from the house or at garden entry points, or they may be part of the sub-axes and subdivisions. As the circulation leads you through the garden you may come across a sub-axis that gives you a glimpse of an eye-catcher – an urn or statue – and you have to decide which way to go.

Each subdivision is a garden in miniature and has its axes and vistas, and quite often its own eye-catchers – a garden building, gazebo, urns, pots, fountain, or seat. The style and character of these features depend on the kind of atmosphere you want to create: a beautiful carpentry seat painted creamy white set against a dark, semi-circular clipped yew hedge will signal a different atmosphere from a rustic bench beneath an apple tree with roses tumbling out of it. Both are intimate spaces but with a very different mood. By substituting either seat with, say, a minimalist stone bench, the mood would be completely altered again.

Seats are always highly atmospheric, but planters are also good for creating and changing mood. Old, weathered terracotta pots and contemporary stainless steel containers offer two extremes. The shape of a container has an important effect too: the curves of a classic urn, whether stone or lead, will give its part of the garden a different sense of place from a stark rectangular container.

Playing against expectation always adds to a garden's excitement. One of the best ways of doing this is the juxtaposition of the old and the new. The effect of putting a contemporary sculpture into an old garden, for example, can be stunning.

top right At Hatfield Palace a double row of *Quercus ilex* lines the main circulation route and draws the visitor to the edge of the terrace to view the rest of the garden.

bottom right Within this kitchen garden goblet apple trees lead to a gazebo. The beautiful structure marks the cross axis and gives height and a focal point to the garden.

top right The terrace at Heale House, Wiltshire has a magical atmosphere because plants have been allowed to self-seed between the stones. They soften the terrace and connect it to the garden.

bottom right In my Lincolnshire garden I have mown a lawn parterre as a subtle way of creating interest in a flat expanse of grass.

right Landscape designer
Kathryn Gustafson has
created a thrilling link to
other parts of a park at
Terrasson-la-Villedieu,
Central France, using a
stepped water chute flanked
by *Salix elaeagnos* ssp.
Angustifolia. The cascade of
rushing water invites further
exploration of the park.

water

Water is one of the most important influences on the mood of a garden and one of the easiest tools for changing the atmosphere. As a significant part of a garden's backbone water has a hugely magnetic pull that draws us through the garden. We can spend hours beside a pond, stream or fountain because water is the life-giver to the garden. Water can either occur naturally, such as a stream or lake, or be a man-made pond, or other feature; or it can be a combination of the two, where a natural stream feeds an artificial pond.

A stream or river that runs through a plot is a natural backbone from which the design of the garden will stem. The water may lead you through the garden, border the property, or be the focal point. Such water brings its own sense of place to a garden, and it is usually unnecessary to add anything except some subtle planting. It is possible to alter the mood of natural water though, by damming or diverting it slightly to form a pond so that the stream flows through a larger body of water. Another subtle device is to submerge a log in shallow water so that it makes a rippling noise as it flows.

Natural water can be enhanced too. At Cranborne Manor in Dorset the water garden is a tiny winter stream that comes in through the fields. The garden originally stemmed from this stream which probably once flowed into ancient fish ponds. Today, the water has been slightly manipulated. It begins as a natural rushing stream that enters a big, man-made pool. It exits into a stream and then pours into a huge fish tank. It is wonderful because the enhancement is so subtle.

Even though you can manipulate nature, you cannot re-create it without a natural water supply. I would never create a fake stream or waterfall. They never feel right. I always feel that such things must be genuine or they do not add a real sense of place to a garden.

Whether still or moving, simple or elaborate, water features can substantially alter the subdivisions of a garden and its atmosphere. Water is a strong element of the backbone and should be linked to vistas and axes and its position has a strong impact. For maximum effect a water feature is usually placed on a crossing point as a centrepiece, or at an end to a vista, and the form it takes dictates the mood. It could be a bowl or urn from which water drips very slowly into a sump of rock with ferns and moss. This creates a meditative sense of place, tranquil, green and timeless, and if approached from a contrasting area of hot planting, can make a dramatic change in mood. The very smell of water and damp is atmospheric.

Water features are also very adaptable. They can be contemporary or traditional or a mix of the two, and either formal or informal. A formal pool with stone edging and a naturalistic pond not only look different, but create an entirely different mood. Moving water, such as a basin of rippling water, a fountain, or a wall of stainless steel or glass over which water pours in a small town courtyard can provide the energy that plants cannot supply because of the lack of space.

Water can also be used as a link between the house and garden or garden and landscape. At Heale House in Wiltshire, there are formal pools and fountains either side of the entrance that mark the way into the house. They also provide interest when inside looking out. Some contemporary houses even have a canal of water that begins inside the house in an atrium or garden room and continues out into the garden beneath a glass wall. And for a link between the cultivated garden and the landscape, try a pond bridging the two.

The reflective qualities of water in the garden were recognized in Europe during the seventeenth century when the great landscape architect André Le Nôtre

above At Parnham House in Dorset, the water rill is a major component of the backbone. It takes the visitor along its route and leads them to mount the steps to the heart of the house.

created water mirrors at Versailles. But you do not have to own a château. A pool will reflect the house or a garden building and will bring light into dark corners of the garden. When water is very close to a house its reflections add a special quality when rippling patterns dapple the ceilings; a beautiful device that can easily be achieved even with a small pond.

A sheet of calm water, like a lily pond, creates a mood that can be altered depending on the depth and clarity of the water: very deep pools are black,

mysterious, disturbing and other worldly; shallow pools are lighter and more playful in mood. And both are different in atmosphere from a duckweed-covered iris-edged country pond. Still water freezes, and can be beautiful in winter.

There is an energy to water that can change atmosphere. A pond can have different moods depending on the amount of movement and sound. Water can drip or pour, but is better if it is not falsely exaggerated. The aim is to create a natural gravitational fall of water even if a pump has to be used. A circular pond with a tiny nozzle that forms a surface-denting ripple is tranquil, while a metre-high jet of water that shoots up and splashes noisily down adds excitement. At Chatsworth in Derbyshire this effect is taken to its apogee in the huge spike of the famous fountain, which is full of power and energy.

Water can be fun, playful and fantastical. Eighteenth-century gardens often had whimsical and playful surprise fountains that soaked unsuspecting visitors. In our award-winning Chelsea Flower Show 2000 garden, Piet Oudolf and I included a series of surprise fountains that spouted suddenly from stainless steel bowls. Water features like these are full of exuberance and show how man loves to influence and manipulate nature.

Of course, water can be treated in a more naturalistic manner too. Pools can be natural, full of frogs and other wildlife. It is also possible to give swimming pools a far more natural treatment than the ugly bright blue rectangles locked in by paving that have been the vogue for so long. They can be beautiful when made like eighteenth-century canals, or plastered grey inside to reflect the sky, or edged in brick. Natural swimming pools can be plant edged, and you can swim with the fish. The water is filtered through sand and reed beds and the garden gains a wonderful feature.

The sound of water is an extremely important element in creating a garden's mood. It can be evocative, calming or exhilarating. Water does not just lie flat or shoot up in fountains, a rill can be made to ripple, burble, splash and murmur when its flow is altered with pebbles, grooves, curves, or vertical pillars. The possibilities are numerous. And the noise of water draws people through a garden too. The sound helps a garden's circulation and sense of mystery and anticipation as you set out to find its watery source.

Water is for lingering by and needs a seat next to it. The seat can be ornate and formal, or simple and unaffected. One of the best examples of a simple seat beside water is at Heale House, where a small, green wooden bench is tucked in a boundary hedge beside a sinuous tributary of the River Avon. Its sense of place

is so powerful that the temptation to sit all day as the water slides by is almost irresistible. Crossing water is a potent experience too, and may involve playing Pooh sticks or dangling feet in water. Bridges, stepping stones, logs and decking are all part of the backbone, and the type of crossing can add greatly to the sense of place: a courtyard flooded with water crossed by slate stepping stones is sophisticated and minimalist.

Some gardens have water features that form a strong backbone for the garden, and create a magical sense of place with a flowing transition from natural to man-made, from formal to informal, and incorporate many moods. At Parnham House in Dorset, a huge lion's mask gushes volumes of fresh spring water that pours into an intriguingly empty stone trough. The water empties out underground and disappears. A short distance away the water bubbles up again and rushes away down a wonderful rill that runs through the garden. It forms a strong backbone as the eye is drawn by the reflective water through topiarized trees, beyond which is a lake. Three different moods are drawn together along one axis – the energy of the gushing spring, the silvery ribbon of rill, and the tranquil water of the lake beyond overhung with trees.

The garden that the eighteenth-century landscape architect William Kent created at Rousham in Oxfordshire, has a wonderful meandering rill that serpentines beneath the branches of a yew trees. Light pierces the yew and illuminates the water on its journey to where it drops into a deep, octagonal dipping pool full of crystal-clear water. (In the eighteenth century a dip in the icy water was supposed to cleanse body and soul.) The rill runs out of the pool into a huge, clear pond full of fish. The design links the energy and tranquillity of water, and could easily be translated into a garden of a more modest scale.

kitchen gardens and orchards

above The functional backbone of this French potager allows ordered beds for fruit, vegetables and flowers. The door is beautifully framed by two peach trees.

far right Across the Atlantic, this North American vegetable garden is carved out of the rocks and forest. Its simple backbone of asymmetrical brick paths and edging tiles is a striking contrast to the wilderness beyond the garden boundary.

In the past, the backbone in a kitchen garden had four beds for crop rotation with a central dipping pool as a source of water. Cross paths met in the centre and there were edge paths and borders against the walls which were often full of flowers for cutting. The south wall had early vegetable beds.

Today's kitchen garden is mostly a mixture of vegetables and flowers. In theory, the backbone is not very different from that of the rest of garden, but in the kitchen garden the backbone stems from the fact that form follows function. The whole plot should, if possible, be on a south-facing gradient, which can enable crops to grow weeks early. The strong axial divisions of the plot are absolutely functional and good organization means that beds can easily be reached for tending and harvesting.

The main backbone of the kitchen garden is the walls, which give it a sense of place by excluding the outside world. Once inside the enclosure many gardeners find the ambience one of the most resonant in the whole garden. The walls change the acoustics slightly and the safety and warmth they bring give the kitchen garden a womb-like security and solitude. You can lose yourself there for hours, alone with the plants, birds and the sky. Hedges, however high just never give the same sense of place as walls.

To give some height and vertical backbone the main paths can have apple tunnels or goblet-trained fruit trees along them. Other permanent backbone planting is used to edge the beds and can include herbs, espaliered fruit, or box hedging.

These days, the kitchen garden does not have to follow tradition and there are many ways to loosen it up. It can even be a potager in the main garden. Any kitchen garden can be enhanced with a decorative feature, such as a piece of sculpture, especially if it is witty, like a giant snail's shell.

A traditional kitchen garden is usually away from the main garden and needs a backbone link between the two such as a pathway through a double row of hazels underplanted with spring flowers.

Orchards are part of the backbone too. They are so traditional that they have wonderful associations with a strong sense of the past. Their calm and tranquillity make them belong anywhere. Traditionally, the trees were planted in regimented rows to form a robust backbone, but they can be planted in a contemporary spiral.

knot gardens, parterres and mazes

The backbone holds the garden together throughout the winter, and a knot garden gives pattern and interest through the coldest months. Knot gardens are quite intricate personal spaces with a very intimate sense of place that is playful, symmetrical and full of pattern and intrigue. They can be personal features that include initials or private symbols. The complexity of a knot garden is almost akin to replicating your inner self in the garden.

Knot gardens can vary from simple, big square blocks of box to the true version in which miniature hedges dip under and over each other to form a knot. Sometimes, hedges twist over each other like ropes woven into interesting patterns. The overall idea is to manipulate plants to create minute spaces within the pattern, and to make an intricate pattern from nature can be hugely enjoyable.

Beds in a knot garden's pattern can be as small as 20cm square so they can be used to show off individual plants. I like to put in little plants that would be lost in a border and which are rare or special or sometimes quite difficult to grow, such as tiny species cyclamen or dog-tooth violets, a wonderful viola or a magical auricula. They turn the knot garden into a collector's cabinet. One of the best knots is at Cranborne Manor in Dorset. It has a wonderful collection of little species plants, each one framed by the hedge of the knot. You can also fill the spaces with one type of plant and my favourite is the wild strawberry. I find these fillings better than the coloured gravels that are sometimes used.

Knots are very formal, especially if they are precisely clipped. They have been used as backbone in the garden since the fifteenth century, but they can be given a more relaxed treatment too. One way is to create a knot garden from wavy box hedges instead of rigorously square-clipped ones, or to use tiny hawthorn hedges infilled with a wild planting, such as cow parsley.

A parterre is pattern on a grand scale and is more like a horticultural brocade, which needs to be viewed from above. Parterres evolved

left The sinuous hedges of a labyrinth maze form a beautiful and playful backbone that also makes a striking backdrop to the delicate but casual planting of water iris.

when the drawing rooms of large houses were on the first floor to avoid the damp, and special gardens were created to be seen from above. In the past, many English gardens also had turf mounts so that the patterns of parterres could be clearly seen.

You can take inspiration from the grandest parterres and scale them down to make more practical and informal versions. Low hedges of box infilled with gentle plumes of lavender give a less formal, loose, fluffy feel. You can even make a parterre with different lengths of grass. A parterre in lime chippings edged with metal and planted with thyme has a more contemporary, minimalist style. Or try a simple parterre of grass or herbs. Do not worry about the traditional patterns, simply create a pattern on the ground. The different scales of knots and parterres: one intimate, intricate, playful and personal, the other more open and on show create contrasting atmospheres.

Mazes also have a wonderful sense of place in which you can, quite literally, lose yourself. There is a great sense of excitement, adventure, challenge and mystery in a maze. They too, create another major part of the backbone in either turf or hedge.

Knots, parterres and mazes involve creating a pattern to give long lasting interest to the backbone, especially through the winter. They also inject fun into the garden. Manipulating nature by clipping and cutting shows off horticultural skills which is, in itself, very atmospheric and symbolic of the journey through life.

top The knot garden here is used to create an area of interest on the upper terrace at Hatfield House. It also helps to unite the distant maze with the garden near the house.

bottom The backbone of this simple garden has been dressed down in a delightfully romantic and informal way. The standard box balls in the knots float in a haze of white forget-me-knots and link with the box balls beneath the young fruit trees.

courtyards and roof terraces

above The backbone of this exuberant green courtyard is formed by the balustrades and the walls of the buildings. It creates a protected enclosure ensuring that the riot of plants can thrive.

far right In San Francisco a roof with a view has minimal planting and a simple backbone of walls in order not to detract from the spectacular view of the Golden Gate Bridge.

If you have ever stood in a hot dark alley in the centre of an old Spanish city and pushed open one of the huge doors, you will know what a glorious surprise is concealed behind its unpromising wooden bulk. As the door swings inward a waft of cool, lemon-scented air escapes. Inside is a green oasis with a gently splashing fountain, pots of citrus plants, pillars and shady seats – it is a courtyard garden.

Courtyards are often spiritual places with an immense sense of place. The pillared cloisters of ancient religious buildings were created to give monks a place to meditate and exercise, and they are still among the most peaceful and atmospheric of courtyard spaces.

There are generally two types of courtyard, one is the internal courtyard found in Tudor (especially Elizabethan), Moorish and Spanish houses. It was formed to let in light and air, and to create a cool outdoor space in the centre of a house. The other is an external courtyard garden. Both are enclosed private spaces with a secure, protected feeling.

A courtyard should be an oasis within a desert and create a glorious sense of surprise. To give the most powerful impact courtyards should be in complete contrast to

their surroundings: in cities they can be meditative spaces that are tranquil, and contemplative. In the country, the contrast is most effective where fields sweep right up to an old farmhouse. When you step from the house there is a gem of a scented courtyard which is packed with lovingly tended plants.

The courtyard effect works in contemporary buildings too, where internal courtyards are often surrounded by glass and give

fence), which unifies the garden by pulling the whole plot together and identifying it as one space.

There are different ways of creating a defining line around your garden and choosing which type depends on the job it needs to do in conjunction with the setting and aspect of the garden. If the boundary is to provide privacy and security or protection from the elements, then it will need to be an enclosure. An invisible boundary, such as a ha-ha, makes the views beyond visible and borrows the landscape by bringing it into the garden. Where more definition is needed then low hedges or long grass at the edge of the garden work well, especially if the garden is bordered by rolling farmland.

Pierced boundaries, such as high hedges with doorways and windows or peepholes cut in, give protection from the elements and tantalizing views of the surrounding countryside. There is an excellent example in the herb garden at Cranborne Manor where an extremely wide, wavy topped hedge seems like an impenetrable fortress, until you stumble on a hole cut in it and can see sheep or cows grazing in the field beyond. Many boundaries are a combination of these different types.

The choice of boundary material is influenced by the architecture of the house, the landscape in which the garden sits, the effect as a backdrop to planting, the style and mood of the garden, and the available local materials. Walls can be of stone or brick using local building techniques, while concrete walls plastered and colour-washed give a contemporary feel.

Hedges make marvellous boundaries and are very adaptable: you can use hawthorn for a wild and informal hedge, and yew for a formal garden. There is an organic fence with great atmosphere at the Welsh Museum in Cardiff, made of big timber posts with ash branches nailed between them, but where you can see through, it is delicate.

Whatever the material, the boundary should give a sense of scale and relate to the scale of the house. High walls around a tiny garden can be dominant and claustrophobic, and small gardens need as much light as possible.

A cottage garden adjoining a cornfield may need a low hedge so that the field is readily visible, even when the owner is sitting down. Adding a gate to a boundary will make a small garden appear to go on. Borrowing the landscape in this way makes the plot seem bigger.

The boundary can change as it goes round the garden. There may be stretches where it needs to be high and dense to act as a screen. In other stretches it can open up to a view. Varying heights act like punctuation, and walls can be further punctuated with finials, hedges with topiary or niches for seats. Nor does a boundary have to be formal and close-trimmed, it can be organic in form. A cloud hedge, cut to resemble the freeform of billowing clouds, adds a feeling of gentleness and maturity. It is particularly useful in giving a new garden a sense of age.

The boundary can create as much atmosphere as the garden itself. A simple hawthorn hedge gives a gentle end to a garden, and if short grass meets long grass at the boundary a garden ends subtly. When you stand at a ha-ha there is a feeling of energy and power.

Boundaries are also a foil for plants, and a dark yew hedge sets off wild planting to perfection, while an old hedge of hawthorn and field maple with primroses beneath is strongly nostalgic in feel. There are magical places either side of boundaries too, with stolen and forgotten spaces where paths wind through long grass under the boughs of overhanging trees.

plant moods

introduction

Combinations of different textures and colours of plants can dramatically alter the mood of a garden. For me, these moods fall into three main categories: tranquil, reflective and relaxing; sumptuous and baroque; vibrant, energizing and stimulating. Pale blues, yellows and pinks, silver, greys and soft greens, whites and creams are the main colours for creating a tranquil mood. A sumptuous and beautifully rich mood is achieved with deep reds, clarets, terracottas, dark purples, copper and bronze, while strong blues and yellows, hot pinks, lime greens and bright oranges and reds are energizing and stimulating.

Different shapes and textures of plants help to create alternative atmospheres too. Gypsophila is airy, transparent and subtle in mood, while a bulky plant with big leaves and flowers creates a mood that is more controlled. Flat flowerheads, such as achillea, that form floating horizontals, are very different in feel from those of irises, which are a less solid and more veil like.

Proportion of colour is also important, as is the number of varieties in combination. A mix of just two plants can be very strong: blue *Nepeta racemosa* 'Walker's Low' and warm red *Achillea* 'Walther Funcke' or *Achillea* 'Terracotta' makes a controlled sense of place and a different mood from a border mixing 12 plants.

When I am working on a garden design I try to put in what I call an undercoat of planting – a plant that runs all the way through the garden and unites it. The undercoat planting should be a colour that goes with any mood and any plant combination making a gentle transition from one part of the garden to another. Tying a garden together can be as simple as using a continuous blue ribbon of chicory. The emphasis and atmosphere can be changed with the scent, texture and colour of the plants that go with the undercoat. Other good undercoat plants are *Nepeta sibirica* or

N. 'Walker's Low', euphorbia, which links herbaceous and shrub gardens so well, and *Verbena bonariensis* – a wonderful purple that goes with different shades of pink and pale yellow, particularly the pale yellow sunflower *Helianthus* 'Valentine'. Seen in soft September light the combination has the most amazing air of calm.

Other plant associations include plants that scramble. *Viola cornuta* has a wonderful habit of clambering up through the base of other plants. If planted beneath old-fashioned roses its smoky blues flower all summer. It relaxes the atmosphere and dresses down the roses softening and calming them with its lacy tapestry.

In large gardens the various rooms can be planted with different plant combinations to create different moods. In small gardens the mood can change with the seasons. Spring might start with lime green *Euphorbia polychroma* with camassias, which would be a fresh, stimulating and yet calm mood. As summer progresses hot pinks and oranges will energize the garden, while autumn could have the sombre richness of claret dahlias and opulent purples of Michaelmas daisies.

If you have a good backbone you can easily change the emphasis in the garden. For the first few years the herbaceous border might be pale blue, silvery grey and white, creating a ghostly, cool, calm garden, particularly in the evenings when the light catches the white flowers. Then you may want a more stimulating mood and change the planting to bright oranges and reds. Such changes can be made on an annual basis too, especially in pots. One year might see green and white tulips with pale blue forget-me-nots or tiny pale blue violas for a calm and tranquil mood. The following year the garden could look and feel quite different with energizing bright orange and pink tulips. Whatever the mood there is always a combination of amazing plants and colours with which to experiment.

page 88/89 French lavender (*Lavandula stoechas*) and *Persicaria bistorta* 'Superba' flower together in a spectacular planting. The simplicity of the plant combination is striking in that it creates a complex mood that has energy and richness, yet at the same time seems beautifully calm.

left A lovely cool planting of white love-in-the-mist (*Nigella damascena*) with lamb's tongue (*Stachys byzantina*), a pale pink old-fashioned rose and a bright yellow verbascum. Although that bright yellow is full of energy the grey leaves of the lamb's tongue match those of the verbascum and draw it into a feminine coolness and calm. The spark of yellow seems to enhance and highlight the calmness.

tranquil, relaxing and reflective

Tranquil planting really can relax people, especially if they have a hectic lifestyle. The calming colours are predominantly pale blue, pale yellow, cream, green, white, lime green, very soft purple and mauve, grey and silver, and the palest pink. All the colours are at the soft end of the palette and seem to have a way of slowing down time and making it stand still, whereas hot colours seem to speed everything up.

right Greys and pale mauves are the colours of the calm spectrum giving an overall feeling of tranquillity to this wonderfully misty scene. Dense clumps of lavender border the path, which is backed by the bottle-brush plumes of persicaria, fluffy-headed eupatorium and the deeply cut leaves of a grey artemesia. The rich purples are dark, sombre and faded and they balance the pale colours well. It is the sort of garden that does not draw you through in a rush, but calms you down and allows you to linger. A day spent in a chair here would pass at a slow, steady pace.

top left A border of violet-blue bellflowers (*Campanula lactiflora* 'Loddon Anna') and pink centaurea, with a backdrop of verbascum and creamy monkshood (*Aconitum* 'Ivorine'), creates a deliberately ordered mood of calm sophistication. It is the epitome of English rectory-style planting.

top right Pink roses and ox-eye daisies tangle together among long grass. The simple planting gives a relaxed atmosphere that mixes a wild, reflective and tranquil quality with the romance of a forgotten garden. The effect is easily created by adding wild flowers to an ordered scheme.

bottom In garden designer Mark Brown's Normandy orchard, a planting of iris, aquilegia and monkshood gives a pervasive mood of tranquillity and reflection.

top Lush, green calm is created with intense blue *Viola sororia* 'Freckles' and the fresh green of a newly shooting fern. The result – all coolness and tranquillity in shades of blue and green.

bottom A late summer calm, very cool and relaxed planting of a wonderful white achillea and the single white *Dahlia* 'Omo' with *Felicia amelloides*. This greeny white planting entices you to sit near on a hot day, pull your sun hat over your eyes and fall asleep.

sumptuous and baroque

This is a rich mood of warm and uplifting calmness. The colours are predominantly deep claret red, rich purple, dusky orange, smoky pink and warm terracotta with bronze and wine-red foliage. These opulent colours have the richness of luxuriant velvet brocade and are often at their best in late summer and early autumn.

left The smoky cinnamon-pink of *Heuchera sanguinea* beneath *Rosa* 'Niles Cochet' gives a calm yet rich feel.

page 98 top left Late spring partners of bright pink tulips (*Tulipa* 'China Pink'), deep mauve perennial wallflower (*Erysimum* 'Bowles Mauve') and the dark *Tulipa* 'Queen of Night'. A spectacular planting that has a deep, baroque richness.

page 98 top right Snapdragons (*Antirrhinum majus*) and sweet William (*Dianthus barbatus* Nigrescens Group) make a wonderfully rich plant combination with dark leaves and deep red flowers that give an opulent, sombre mood.

page 98 bottom An arresting contemporary combination of the rust-coloured *Iris* 'Kent Pride', and a stunning lipstick-pink foxglove.

page 99 top A delectable waterside planting of the buttery yellow giant marsh marigold *Caltha palustris* and dark copper-red *Astilbe* x *Arendsii*.

page 99 bottom left Purple salvia and burnt orange *Helenium* 'Wyndley' backed by white gypsophila has great richness and depth, and is like a piece of exquisite Jacobean brocade.

page 99 bottom right Alliums, aquilegias and poppies in deep plums and dark blues make a sumptuous yet naturalistic planting.

vibrant, stimulating and energizing

Energizing plants are good for changing the pace in a garden, especially if you are fortunate enough to have a large garden where you can create different rooms. A vibrant planting is very stimulating after a calm green area and makes a contrast with woodland or a water meadow beyond the boundary. This plant mood can also suit a small garden where the owner just wants a vibrant atmosphere. It can either match a dynamic interior or contrast with a calm setting inside the house. Plants for this mood are mostly reds, oranges, yellows and some dark blues.

right A powerful early autumn planting of dahlias and *Crocosmia* x *crocosmiiflora* in hot orange that has huge energy. It conjures up memories of childhood harvest festivals and vegetable gardens brimming with crops. The mood associations are very strong and recall the smell of ripening apples in an Indian summer of warmth and sunshine.

left An electric blue delphinium with a ruby red daylily together in a positive and exuberant display.

far right, top left Spring vibrancy with a fabulous combination of an ornamental pink cherry and bright orange crown imperials with their black stems. The colours are stimulating, but the contrasting shapes of the delicate bough of the cherry above the crown imperials and their tufted green top-knots adds huge energy.

far right, top right The intense yellow of a daylily and *Anthemis tinctoria* spiked with plumes of purple lavender, backed by lime-green tobacco plants and white marguerites give this planting great vibrancy.

far right, bottom Orange annual Californian poppies with a rich red perennial poppy (*Papaver* 'Fireball) and *Potentilla* 'Flamenco' make a thrilling combination. The dynamic reds and oranges reflect the mood of a hot summer in the garden.

garden
objects

introduction

Garden objects are the punctuation points in the garden and are placed to mark a route, view or boundary and create extra interest. They take a variety of forms from urns, containers and plant supports to benches, sundials, fountains, gates and statues. Accessories do not have to be expensive: sculpture from a local art exhibition can work just as well as a Henry Moore, and a piece of driftwood found on a shoreline can make a beautiful feature.

One of the main functions of garden objects is to aid circulation in the garden by encouraging you to approach and look at them. They are signposts that mark the way to a new route. Placed on an axis, accessories such as a fountain, sundial, or statue can mark a cross-axis showing an alternative way through the garden. Urns might be used to mark steps or a gate into another part of the garden.

Objects can also give a pause or breathing space, and so change the pace of the garden. An urn set in a niche in a hedge, or a sundial on a sunny lawn, make the visitor pause and take stock of the garden. And a statue or piece of contemporary sculpture, a seat or a gate can be used to terminate a route or mark the garden boundary, or indicate an exquisite view beyond.

Setting an accessory in the right place is extremely important as it adds to the sense of place. A well-weathered wooden table with seats placed among trees can enhance a reflective, calm mood in the garden. A bench in a hidden corner offers privacy and secrecy, a place to reflect or read, but the same bench moved to an open lawn, where the sitter can look back at the house, has a different sense of place, it is an invitation for others to join the sitter.

Choosing a piece depends on the owner, and the setting and mood of the garden. Contemporary fountains, gates and sculpture can be commissioned from craftsmen and artists, or the hunt may be on (and it can take years) for an antique piece. Junk shops and architectural salvage yards yield great finds that need not break the budget. An old chair may look exactly right under a tree, or a bashed stone column can come into its own when topped with the right urn or pot. For a minimal approach you just need one exquisite lead, zinc or oak container, carefully placed, to give a restrained sense of place. Whatever the taste, the impact is lost if there are too many accessories: one gem is far more effective than a jumble of ornaments.

Garden objects also include lighting, but I tend to steer away from electric lights. I only use them in an extremely gentle and subtle way to highlight focal points and I prefer not to light paths or whole gardens. When light is needed I use candle lanterns hung in trees as they create a much more subtle and romantic atmosphere than an electric light.

New or old, accessories should always enhance the atmosphere. A stainless steel fountain of gushing water bursts with energy, whereas an old stone fountain covered with moss invites reflection. A lichen and moss-covered statue with a chipped nose and part of an arm missing exudes atmosphere with a deep feeling of age and can add antiquity to a new garden.

page 104/105 Garden objects should never be purely ornamental. The value of accessories like this rhubarb forcer, and kale forcers, line winders, cloches and old garden tools, is that they have a practical function. I love pulling the lid off this rhubarb forcer in my Lincolnshire garden, and plucking out the new, fresh rhubarb.

left In an Italian garden a handmade terracotta pot with a lemon tree sits in front of a large statue holding a cornucopia. These two quite different objects punctuate and add a different texture to the box hedges and topiarized yew that surround them. They also draw the visitor through the garden, and at the same time make a dramatic pause in the mass of topiary and lighten the mood. Large statues can be used in quite small gardens, so never be afraid to be bold. They can create great impact as long as the planting is scaled to match the boldness of the piece.

the finishing touches

top right A wonderful mellow oak bench at Great Dixter in East Sussex, placed against a yew hedge at the end of a vista. It provides a reflective, peaceful mood and, once you have walked through the garden, is the place to head for. You can sit and look back along the vista, remembering all you have seen. Set on York stone paving, backed by the dark yew and facing long, wild grass, it is inviting and perfectly balanced. The scale of the seat is bold enough to make a statement against the power of the yew hedge.

bottom right Plant supports are extremely useful for creating height in the garden. They may be as simple as hazel branches tied in a wigwam for supporting sweet peas, or more ornamental metal arches and even fruit cages. At the Villa Pisani in Italy, a simple rusting rose arch forms the backbone and vista of this garden. The arch leads the eye right through with an unmissable invitation to enter the perfumed tunnel and explore the romantic garden.

far right At Castle Drogo, Devon, Edwin Lutyens designed this wonderfully atmospheric gate with a powerful sense of arrival and departure. The valley and the trees beyond are echoed in the V at the top of the gate and in its vertical posts, linking it strongly to the landscape.

right A stone column sundial contrasts with the rich earth red of Wyken Hall in Suffolk. The sundial punctuates and gives height, texture and form to a little knot garden. Sundials are best set on lawns or paths in rose gardens where, as long as it is sunny, they can be read. They suit tranquil situations, with billowing roses and lavender, because they symbolize eternity and a calm way of life. Sundials have a feel-good factor as they are associated with sunshine.

far right A frosty early spring morning in my Lincolnshire kitchen garden and the sun catches the well-worn handle of my line winder that marks a straight row ready for planting. Old tools like this are a marvellous link to the past. The plant label sticking out of the soil is made from off-cuts of edging boards that I designed for my physic garden. Although I don't use them else-where, labels are very important in the kitchen garden as they record the date and variety of plants. At the end of each season I collect them up and seal them in a box so that I have a record of what I planted and experimented with that year.

left Wind-sculpted trees are a great inspiration. For a Scottish garden I designed beech topiary hedges in the shape of wind-sculpted trees that echoed the shapes of the windswept landscape beyond. The topiary fitted well with the surroundings and tied the garden back into the landscape, making it at one with nature.

a natural bay with a little gravel spit, and so nature provides the basis of design for a seamless boundary to a new lake or pond.

Fast-flowing clear streams and rivers have a very different atmosphere from a shady pool or pond covered in duckweed. I knew both as a child and refer to them often. When I want to create a gentle and relaxed area of water in a garden I introduce duckweed and water iris. I love streams, especially streams in woods with clear, rushing water and little pools surrounded by moss-covered rocks, with ferns dipping down and the reflection of overhead branches. The way water moves – trickling from one pool to another or gushing over rocks – influences how I create a symbiosis of nature and cultivation in a garden. I try to make features as natural as possible so that they fit in with

left In Dorset I have seen marvellous natural roadside plant combinations of pink valerian with ox-eye daisies. Because they have not been sprayed for seven years these flowery Dorset verges have bluebells, red campion and wild garlic forming a natural herbaceous border. They are natural plant combinations that can be used in a garden.

nature, especially the landscape beyond the boundary. I always try to emulate nature's perfect balance – rocks, moss and ferns round streams for example – and I try to capture its timelessness.

Wind-sculpted trees and natural plant combinations are also important references. In Germany verge spraying was stopped several years ago and now the natural plant combinations by the roadside are amazing. I remember one had claret-coloured sanguisorbas and blue geraniums with wild achilleas and grass – all wild plants. It was extraordinarily beautiful. The garden I designed for The Wildlife and Wetland Trust at Barnes in west London was influenced by the natural plant combinations on that roadside.

Many plantspeople collect plants from the wild under license to get the right combinations and good plant stock. The North American wild prairie plantings of echinaceas and grasses make an excellent effect for a drive or a huge herbaceous border. It is really important to look at nature and see what it does. Its plant combinations are inspirational and it balances the shape, texture and size of different plants so well.

man-made

Attempts to tame nature and create features in it are another important part of my visual directory. They include the way man has carved and managed the landscape into fields, woodland, water, and moorland. It also includes coppicing to harvest timber that has the added bonus of allowing dormant plants to grow.

This taming of nature influences the way I think about gardens. Man has a wonderful ability to turn nature's raw materials, such as clay or stone, into many things from the bricks for a wall to a stone finial. Topiary and pleaching are forms of sculpting trees that connect nature with our own individual sense of place.

I love topiary because it is a direct connection to the past – the wonderful art and craft of creating sculpture in green. Topiary makes a magical composition of wild against tame if it is set in wild flower meadows. Grown among the formality of roses, topiary does not have the same impact. Long meadow grass punctuated with topiary is how I imagine Tudor gardens must have looked. Without lawn mowers there were no lawns as we know them, and the grass was allowed to grow into flowery meads that were scythed once or twice a year. It is a look that can be very contemporary, and inspires and influences the gardens that I create.

Trained fruit trees and roses trained along walls also influence the way I design. I find them timeless: they look as good in a contemporary garden as they do in a traditional English one. At Rousham House in Oxfordshire there is a wonderful apple walk underplanted with Barnhaven primulas, wallflowers and tulips. Its atmosphere is powerful and one that I frequently try to capture in my gardens.

Manipulating nature is a recurring theme of my work. Walks of pleached trees, especially hornbeams and lime trees, have been made for hundreds of years. They are a lovely balance of human scale and proportion. Lines

above At Great Dixter, Sussex, the topiaried yew trees have an amazing sense of scale. The clipped and formal topiary is rooted into a carpet of wild flower meadow with a backdrop of huge trees. The contrast between nature and man-made is made stronger through association.

of pleached trees refer to the past, but work just as well in a contemporary urban courtyard with abstract sculpture, or a single tree at its centre.

Dry-stone walls form an abstract pattern on the British landscape, and I find the divisions of these functional walls a marvellous reference. There are so many points to pick up on: the shapes, the pattern of the laid stones, and the way nature furnishes them with moss and ferns make a fabulous combination that can be used in a garden. Old walls are almost works of art. I might make a dry-stone-wall maze in a wood as a surprise focal point. Other man-made features in natural settings, such as a rill in a wood or an ancient stone circle in moorland or meadow, are also inspirational, exciting and full of energy.

Old potting sheds have also long been a significant influence. When you push the door open it squeaks on its hinges and inside is a treasure house of old tools and

as
od.

top left William Kent's urn at Rousham House, Oxfordshire, encapsulates the spirit of his classical garden design 1737–1741. It has been a constant inspiration for capturing the essence of eighteenth-century gardens.

top right The sinuous ripple of water in this beautifully simple man-made rill in a wood at Château de Saint-Just, France, is compelling. The narrow rill, bordered by very straight moss-covered stone, has energy in the stillness of the wood.

bottom left Richard Harris's sculpture uses materials from its woodland setting to great effect. It has a Bronze Age, pagan feel of bold monoliths and woodland spirits, evocative of childhood forest camps.

rhubarb forcers. Potting sheds brim with atmosphere. Warm and balmy, they have an evocative smell of Jeyes fluid, creosote, garden twine and earth. A potting shed is the factory of the garden, a place to generate plants and sow seed, and the inner sanctum and a place of refuge on a cold wet day when the rain beats down on a tin roof. Wherever possible I put them into gardens that I create, even modern gardens.

I also love kitchen gardens because they involve growing, cooking and eating good organic food. For me, the kitchen garden at Hanford School in Dorset, where my godmother taught, was particularly influential. I was the only child allowed inside, so it was a very special place. It was soaked in the secret and mysterious atmosphere of Frances Hodgson Burnett's *The Secret Garden*. At the age of six or seven I loved to wander through its vegetables and huge herbaceous borders of cutting flowers, the wonderful greenhouses with agapanthus, lilies, azaleas and citrus trees in pots. I was forbidden to go in the potting shed, but of course I used to sneak in when Mr Underwood, the gardener, was not looking and stare in fascination at the rhubarb forcers and wonder why they were not used any more. When I asked Mr Underwood, he explained all the traditional methods of growing rhubarb.

Although smell is invisible, it has to be one of the greatest influences on me. Perfume is so evocative and adds greatly to a garden's atmosphere. Lily of the valley is a favourite, as are regale lilies. They are reminiscent of sitting out in the sun at peace with the garden. Half-decaying fallen apples have an extremely evocative smell too, and recall autumn. I plant apple trees for their blossom and fruit, and also for their wonderful appley smell. Among the scented plants too numerous to list herbs have an equally important place, and I frequently use them in gardens to enhance the atmosphere.

above Perfume in the garden is very evocative. I often use viburnums and daphnes, especially *Daphne odora*. They have associations with growing up in perfumed gardens. *Viburnum carlesii* 'Diana' (above) has a really sweet, powerful fragrance.

top right To lie in the middle of a stone circle is incredible. The energy, the sense of the pagan and the mists of prehistory generate an atmosphere that I try to emulate in the garden. Castlerigg Stone Circle near Keswick in Cumbria is a fine example of the power and significance of stone circles.

bottom right A lovely old espalier apple tree forms a boundary to a path in a French potager. It is an example of how we can manipulate nature. Bordering a flowerbed and delineating the garden's backbone, it gives significant structural elements that would be missing if it grew in its natural form. One apple tree like this can spark off dozens of variations of ideas of form, screening and garden m

art, architecture and gardens

There is such a rich panoply of art, architecture and gardens to draw on, that making a selection for this visual directory is more frustrating than choosing eight Desert Island Discs. Fortunately, in the real world, my portfolio of reference can encompass a massive range whereas here I only have room to concentrate on the architecture, the houses and the gardens, pictures and textiles about which I am most passionate.

Of all the houses and gardens I know, Cranborne Manor in Dorset has the most perfect sense of place. The medieval hunting lodge and Jacobean manor on Cranborne Chase, which I visited almost every week when I was young, has been a seminal influence.

The garden was created by John Tradescant, gardener to James I, for the Cecil family in the seventeenth century. Many varieties of plants came in from all over the world to make it. It still has that sense of newness and excitement that it must have had when it was first created, and when I visit I come away with that feeling. The garden itself is laid out in a traditional English manner on a domestic scale with a lime walk, yew *allée*, wonderful lawn with a revolving tennis house, a memorable kitchen garden, an intricate knot garden and beautiful wild-flower meadows.

It has always had a very strong backbone, but it was never manicured. The planting is wonderfully loose and the plants are allowed to grow in their own way spilling out on to paths and scrambling up trees. The smallest part would make a garden in its own right. Among these features are the mount in the rose garden, the daisy-strewn croquet lawn, which taught me that lawns can have character, and the windows cut in the thick yew hedges to view the meadows beyond.

There are several other English houses and gardens that have had a significant influence on me. They include Parnham House, also in Dorset, which is more masculine than Cranborne, with bold lines, rills and topiary, Heale House and Corsham Court in Wiltshire; Blickling Hall, Norfolk; Rousham House, Oxfordshire; Ham House, Surrey and Hatfield House in Hertfordshire.

As a child I went on picnics to the ruins of Wardour Castle in Dorset. I could never work out why. I loved the main doorway at Wardour with its lions' heads and lozenge shapes. Years later I learned that it had been altered by Robert Smythson, the architect who lived in the late-sixteenth and early-seventeenth centuries. I find Smythson's work a great inspiration, especially the decorative detail in his designs for doorways and fireplaces. Each time I look at his work (and also at architectural pattern books of the period) I get an idea for a project. The designs lend themselves to many types of garden from the historic to the minimalist.

Tumbledown garden pavilions, grottoes and temples, lichen-encrusted statues and moss-covered urns that are crumbling in romantic decay are great influences on my work, especially where nature has taken over so that they have become like living Piranesi sculpture. They are an amalgam of a sense of history, excitement and decaying beauty. To me they are more glorious in their decayed form than when they were new and grand in their heyday. They also have a secret garden quality – that wonderful sense of the stumbled upon – that makes them extremely special.

The Italian Renaissance painter Piero della Francesca is another great favourite. I often use the earthy colours of his paintings in planting schemes or on the walls of contemporary gardens. Among twentieth-century painters the work of Paul Klee, Ben Nicholson and Marc Chagall are a constant source of inspiration. The colours, forms and atmospheres of their paintings trigger many ideas for planting schemes, grass parterres and changes of mood in gardens.

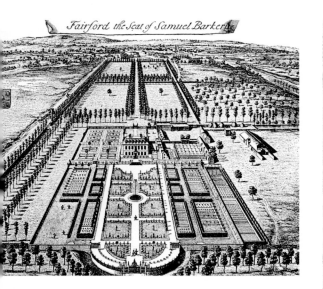

Fairford the Seat of Samuel Barker

far left, top In the eighteenth century many great houses and their gardens were drawn by Jan Kip, the Dutch engraver. Kip recorded many features, such as parterres, mazes and wilderness gardens, which give me the beginning of ideas for both contemporary and more traditional gardens.

far left, bottom My favourite picture is Leonardo da Vinci's charcoal and chalk drawing *The Virgin and Child with Saint Anne and Saint John the Baptist*. I always get a feeling of comfort and security from it, but each time I gaze at it I learn something new. I love the simplicity of the sepia and brown colours and although the composition is strong, it flows and all the lines seem to meld into each other. The picture has an energy and peace that I try to achieve in a garden.

top left The arts, and craft of all kinds fuel my imagination. The starting point is likely to be an embroidery like this mid-seventeenth-century sampler. The geometric patterns are marvellous inspirations for knot gardens. They are so evocative of the past but could easily be used in a contemporary garden.

bottom left The entrances to Heale and the oversized door-way on to the terrace with its plant-filled interces are a rich vein of ideas. One of my favourite places is the kitchen garden with its apple tunnel, box balls and dipping pool.

chelsea flower show 2000

The garden that I designed with Piet Oudolf for The Chelsea Flower Show 2000 drew together many significant influences from my visual directory. The idea was not to make a copy of an historic garden but to create a garden that looked to the future while having its roots in the past. The catalyst for the design was the sense of place that we wanted to create – tranquil yet energizing, with a feeling of mystery and surprise. Above all, it was a marriage of the past and the future. We called it 'Evolution' because the garden progressed from antiquity to the present day.

The mesmerizing ripple pool at the front of the garden grew from the idea of a Roman hot tub. The thought of a hot spring gave two concepts: spring as a starting point, and water as the source of life. The water in the stainless steel bowl moved gently all the time in a sensuous and spiritual way and had a mystic quality.

The pool was surrounded by a soft veil of *Deschampsia caespitosa* and *Iris sibirica* 'Perry's blue' because we wanted the planting to be naturalistic, and took our inspiration from water meadows. The planting was loose and blew in the wind, contrasting with the more formal planting in the large beds.

The ripple pool and the fountains were made by stonemason James Elliot. Near the pool was a modern interpretation of a classic garden bench – an old love seat – carved by Jim Partridge from a solid block of oak and then burnt to get a wonderful black patina.

The inspiration for the colour scheme of the borders came from a Persian carpet. We decided our planting should have the same marvellous dark colours – chocolatey, rich, sombre and peaceful, but full of energy. We used mainly *Astrantia major* 'Claret', *Salvia* x *sylvestris* 'Mainacht', *Viola cornuta*, *Cimicifuga* var. *simplex* Atropurpurea Group, *Euphorbia dulcis* 'Chameleon' and *Centranthus ruber* var. *coccineus*.

The distinctive cloud hedges on either side of the garden evolved from the ancient hedges of English gardens such as Corsham Court, Wiltshire, where they are gnarled, bobbly and full of character. Our box hedge held the sides and cradled the rest of the garden in comforting arms.

The main paths were of limestone chippings. It was a garden material much used in the eighteenth century, but looks very contemporary. Classic gardens used to have statues to represent the seasons but in the Chelsea garden we used four fountains. They were stainless steel dishes with a spout of water that shot intermittently from one to another. At Chelsea they were a great attraction and drew crowds in anticipation. When the fountains spouted everyone laughed, especially when they caught someone on the paths.

The axes running down the centre ended in a clean, crisp, contemporary semi-circular wall that emanated from modern minimalist designs. The colour of the wall was inspired by the reds in the planting, and tied the scheme together throughout, from the red thistle *Cirsium rivulare* 'Atropurpureum' at the front, through to the red astrantias in the formal beds.

In front of the wall were three big monolith fountains of a Lincolnshire stone called Ancaster Weatherbed. They echoed the great pillars of stone found in ancient stone circles. Water poured down the stone monoliths as a reminder that nothing can survive without it. Beneath the monoliths, the water ran into a rectangular pool which was covered in duckweed. The contrast between that and the crisp lines of the fountain, the ancient hedge and the contemporary stone gave the garden immense energy.

above The stainless steel bowls set in box were an interpretation of the surprise joke fountains that soaked visitors in seventeenth- and eighteenth-century gardens. Their unexpected jets of water created a sparkling interaction between Chelsea visitors and the garden and added a human dimension with lots of humour.

far left, left The inspiration for the colours of the planting came from an antique carpet that covered the table in a Dutch pub, just as they did in paintings by seventeenth-century Dutch Masters.

far left, right The matched topiary yew trees were influenced by the ancient cedars found in English gardens. The red wall behind them echoed the planting scheme and became the perfect backdrop for these distinctive trees.

case studies

introduction

The five case studies in this chapter, although very different, exemplify the way in which I approach the making of a garden. They draw together the different elements that compose a sense of place, but range from a town garden in the heart of London to a wildlife garden set in a wetland park, to my own garden in the Fens of Lincolnshire. Each case study covers the fundamental tools that I use in garden design. They include the important influence of the landscape beyond the boundary; the link between the house and garden (where appropriate); the owners and their wish list; the foundation blocks and the backbone of the design; the plant moods; the visual directory or influences; the garden objects and how the garden is to be used. In each case I show how the components come together to form a harmonious whole.

The mood that is created by drawing all these elements together is unique to each garden. What the elements are, and how they are arranged, help to form the sense of place, whether that is tranquil and reflective, ancient and spiritual or full of energy. In creating the sense of place for each garden I have had to modify the existing foundation blocks. I have also had to decide how far to go with my new design; knowing when to stop so that the garden is not overdone is as important as knowing what to include.

page 132/133 In my Lincolnshire garden the lavender either side of the main axis path draws you through to classic urns that mark steps between the herbaceous garden and the pleached lime walk.

left The approach to my house is through cornfields that sweep right up to the windows. There is no formal garden on this side of the house and so there is a strong link between house and landscape.

Once I have gathered the information and established what sort of mood the owner wants to create, I have to refer to the most important and fundamental aspect of all: the overall sense of place and how the garden links to the house and the landscape beyond. It is only when this has been established that the garden can be subdivided into moods, and the designing can really begin.

All the case studies here are imbued with the feeling that, once in the garden, time passes by unheeded and the world beyond can be easily forgotten. My Fenland garden (page 162) has an overall sense of safety, serenity and protection, but each room within it has its own distinct mood. The Urban Green garden (page 144) is a surprise and not what is usually expected of a town garden: it has a sense of escapism and is a reaction against the hectic bustle beyond its walls. Its strong architectural design and planting has an almost masculine feel. The Rus in Urbe garden (page 150) is much more feminine and has a timeless, established quality as if it has been in place for years. It seems as if it is rooted to the spot and that the house has grown out of the garden site, although it is a relatively new garden and was created from scratch only five years ago.

The plot surrounding the Norfolk mill (page 136) is a garden of Eden, and its nucleus is one of peace and tranquillity that marries with the landscape beyond the boundary. The Wildlife and Wetland Trust garden (page 156) is different because it sits within 105 acres of public space in west London. Its magnetic and energetic quality brings mystery and a strong spiritual feel to an enormous green space in one of the world's biggest cities. All the gardens have a gentle and reassuring heartbeat that ensures their sense of place.

a norfolk mill garden

My first memory of this enchanting mill is the approach to it. Driving along little lanes through verdant Norfolk countryside the whole area felt very forgotten: gravel lined the middle of the road, washed there by the rain, with tufts of grass and weeds growing in it – clearly very little traffic passed that way. The lanes were sunk between high, steep banks with hedges on top. Where the meadows were visible they were full of wonderful flowers, and occasionally there was a glimpse of the mill stream as it threaded through the valley. Straight away there was a powerful ambience of an isolated, protected, calm pace of life, especially as the narrow, winding lanes slowed vehicles almost to a walking pace.

Under a wonderful bridge, with arches that looked Roman, the church tower and the manor house appeared among the trees, and then there was a plain five-bar gate and a gravel drive with daisies up the middle that led to the mill. The feeling was relaxed and informal, and the silver thread of the stream drew you on. The drive through the wonderful lanes had set up great anticipation of the arrival at the house. The mill itself nestled in a gently sloping valley, a lovely basin surrounded by ancient beech, oak and luxuriant willows. It was hidden, secret and intimate.

With an approach laden with atmosphere and the surrounding beautiful countryside there was already an intense sense of place. The mill was mentioned in the *Domesday Book* of 1087, and there has been a mill here ever since. Of all the case studies the mill had the most delicate sense of place and I had to take great care not to diminish it. That atmosphere had to be preserved at all costs.

I worked in close collaboration with the owner. My brief was to create new parts of the garden without destroying the harmony between the house, garden, and the landscape beyond. The work was

a complicated and delicate balance as it would have been easy to go too far and we had to know when to stop. The owner and I wanted to wake the garden up a bit, but we did not want to wake it up too much.

The mill house sits astride the millrace and is completely enveloped in roses, rather like a sleeping beauty in a forgotten world. Although the house is a strong feature it appears to have been taken over by roses such as 'Félicité Perpétue'. Inside it is very eclectic with a gentle feel. The colours are light and fresh with pale blues and creams, and the whole ambience is personal and artistic, not one created by a designer. There is a strong New England influence in the furniture and objects but the house is not cluttered, and there is a marked sense of order. Hundreds of books line the shelves including many on travel and there are many beautiful old black and white photographs of Venice.

The overall size of the plot is about eight acres with a lot of wild woodland and a cultivated area of about two and a half acres, but much of that is lawn and orchard. Only about three quarters of an acre is highly structured. My work was done in phases and we are still working on it. The first part of the garden that we tackled was the courtyard in front of the house. It was a gravel car park and from the windows of the house all that could be seen were parked cars and a large beech tree. My brief was to move the car park behind the barn and create a garden in its place, a change that increased the sense of place and built up the anticipation of what might lie beyond.

The new garden was an opportunity to establish a strong entrance to the house and garden, and I created what is really an outside entrance hall, known as the courtyard garden. I did not want it to look as if it had just been made, but to look established, and rooted in

right The mill house is enveloped with roses that scramble and tumble in a free way tying it closely to the wildness of of the woods nearby.

p139, top In the courtyard, the knot garden gives a strong backbone that creates an interesting arrival at the house throughout the year.

p139, bottom Wading through plants that spill across the approach to the courtyard slows the pace down and allows visitors to become at one with the plants.

key to lawn garden

1 herbaceous border
2 grass path
3 grass and lavender planting
4 scarlet oak
5 brick platform
6 pleached hornbeam
7 *Quercus ilex* sentinels
8 yew hedge

the past, in sympathy with the mill. I also wanted it to have a strong organic feel, as the mill does with its wooden railings and clapper boards.

In harmony with the historic origins of the house I began by designing a big knot garden to echo medieval gardens and root the garden in tradition. The knot is a formal geometric pattern influenced by a love of pattern and the owners' love of Venice, where there is so much pattern and formality. The highly structured design of the knot also highlights the contrast with the surrounding countryside.

The backbone took shape when the plot was divided by paths. They are punctuated with stout posts inspired by Venetian gondola posts which, with the oak edging boards of the beds, echo the wooden railings on the mill. There is also an oak gate opening on to a path that creates a long axis to the house. The hand-made brick path ends at furniture maker Paul Anderson's *Three Graces* seat against the house wall, which is covered with honeysuckle and *Garrya elliptica*. The use of oak adds to the intense sense of place.

Box hedging and topiary yew spirals form the backbone planting in this courtyard garden. It is formal and has a strong structure throughout the year but looks especially wonderful on frosty winter mornings. As the courtyard garden is seen from the drawing room, library, kitchen and bedrooms we wanted as many winter flowers as possible, and planted hellebores under the dappled shade of the big beech tree. I also wanted to temper the formality of the knot with a rather wild style of planting that echoes the woods beyond the boundary, and used wild strawberries and *Aquilegia vulgaris* 'William Guiness', a lovely dark claret, between the little box hedges. Around the knot there are beds with hellebores, pale blue iris, tree peonies that flower a burnt orange, ferns, white foxgloves and *Geranium phaeum* and *Astrantia major*. Along the path to the gate is *Geranium clarkei* 'Kashmir Purple' and the claret *rosa* 'Cardinal de Richelieu' with the black-blue flag iris 'Superstition' and more *Aquilegia vulgaris* 'William Guiness'. As you enter the garden the plant mood is rich, vibrant and sombre, moving to cool green in the centre.

Once visitors had been persuaded to park by the barn the routes back to the house had to be improved. The next phase of the garden therefore meant developing the lawn garden in the space between the barn and the house, so that it was as strong as the courtyard garden. The lawn garden is now the starting point of routes to different parts of the whole garden.

above When a lovely garden object is placed in a setting that is right for it the combination can be special. Here, a seat by the furniture maker Paul Anderson is set above the mill race making the perfect place to contemplate the garden.

far right In the lawn garden the soft planting of the grass *Deschampsia caespitosa* makes a wonderful natural foil for the verbascums and salvias and a powerful link with the meadow grasses in the fields beyond the boundary.

It also links back to the courtyard garden across the stream and forms the new route to the house. The links throughout the garden are made harmonious by repeating the key features – the brick paths, oak posts and picket fences, the seats and edging boards, and the box hedging. In fact, there is box in all the cultivated and formal parts of the garden.

The foundation block of the lawn garden was a central scarlet oak (*Quercus coccinea*) and, along one side, the barn, now a studio where the owner writes. There were established beds of old-fashioned roses that were wonderful for two weeks of the year but looked a mess for the rest, so we made the bold decision to take them out. The oak tree became the focal point around which the plot was now divided by

an axis and sub-axes. Grass paths surround a square of hand-made bricks punctuated with beds under the oak in the centre. Beyond the grass are beds formed between the patterns of miniature box hedging. In place of the old roses I planted a little glade of closely spaced beech trees. They will never get really big, but they look wonderful in both winter and summer.

The lawn garden is open to a view of hills beyond the boundary and this influenced my planting plan here. I used the grass *Deschampsia caespitosa*, delphiniums, lupins, lavender, catmint (*Nepeta racemosa* 'Walker's Low') and lady's mantle (*Alchemilla mollis*) – all mainly in soft colours using pale yellows, whites and pale blues. Under the oak are apricot *Verbascum* 'Helen Johnson' and purple *Salvia* x

sylvestris 'Mainacht'. All this is wrapped in the green of a yew hedge, with holm oak (*Quercus ilex*) as sentinels and pleached hornbeams to define the corners.

On the other side of the mill we planted a cloud hedge to envelop and enclose a lawn, and to make a small green room next to the terrace. The cloud hedge forms a strong link to the woods beyond and softens the transition from terrace to woodland.

From the lawn garden a gently undulating daisy lawn goes down to the stream. We left the other side of the stream natural. The flowering in this part of the garden begins with snowdrops and is then full of wild comfrey and garlic under willows and alders. It is managed simply to keep down brambles and other invasive plants, but apart from that is left natural.

On the edges of the garden we planted wild apples, and we let the grass grow longer where it meets the fields. Where the garden meets the woods we planted oak and beech to meld with the woodland species.

The next phase of development was the creation of a small potager near the barn. I wanted to pick up all the references in the garden so that there were recognizable features drawing the garden together. The potager has beds edged with oak boards like those in the courtyard garden, and I designed oak fruit cages for it. Around the perimeter of the potager runs an oak picket fence. This type of open fencing is ideal in situations where an area needs to be defined, but not solidly enclosed. To soften the picket fence I planted a low box hedge in front of it.

The mill garden always had a balance between formality and nature, and this delicate equilibrium has been preserved. The sense of place is still one of mesmerizing calm, and people just want to linger in it. The stream that runs through has little bridges over it with benches where people can sit, and this adds to the soft, flowing, subtle and tranquil sense of place.

far left The willow frame for sweet peas later in the summer echoes the vertical spikes of the *Verbascum* 'Helen Johnson' and adds height beneath the oak tree in the centre of the lawn garden.

top left At the end of a mown path in the orchard flower meadow a sundial is set on the main axis. The axis runs right through to the centre of the courtyard creating a powerful link between two parts of the garden.

top right Decorative fruit cages protect the ripening fruit and frame central beds of herbs and vegetables in the potager.

urban green

Stepping from a busy London street with many parked cars, the transition through the tall gate into the green front garden of this house is quite powerful. The visitor passes through a screen of hornbeams and immediately enters a calm, peaceful, Zen-like atmosphere, which is a great contrast to the surrounding city life. And it was this calm mood that the owner wished to create in the garden at the rear of the house.

It is a typical tall London town house. Set in a street of similar houses, it has a white stucco front that is quite formal whereas the rear is brick and more relaxed, with a great sense of seclusion and peace. Once inside the house it is apparent that the owner is artistic. Wonderful photographs line the walls, and a fragment of a painting and an old artist's palette lean against a mantelpiece. There are pieces of contemporary ceramic, and Duncan Grant tiles and pottery. It has a warm, lived-in atmosphere, full of objects and pictures that reflect the owner's life and the things she loves. A soft light filters through linen curtains and, although there are no bright colours, the house is full of character and has a peaceful, eclectic mood. The garden at the back had to reflect that quality.

The back garden was 1920s in style, enclosed by a wall with raised flower beds around a long rectangular lawn ending in a semi-circle that made it look almost like a swimming pool. The plot measured 14m wide by

right The main axis is the central lawn which I edged with a solid platform of serpentine box hedging with holm oaks (*Quercus ilex*) rising from it to add vertical interest.

key

1 serpentine lawn
2 lead urns with *Trachelospermum jasminoides*
3 copper beech platform
4 semi-circular bench in box hedge
5 pear tunnel
6 standard *Quercus ilex*
7 box serpentine platform
8 fountain
9 pleached limes
10 plant support for *Rosa* 'Tuscany Superb'

far left The solid serpentine platform of box is pierced with *Quercus ilex* sentinels to add vertical interest and to keep the garden looking good throughout the winter.

right The owner of this London house wanted structure, organization and winter interest in the garden as it is viewed from many rooms in house, mostly from above. In the curves of the serpentine hedging I added large lead containers planted with star jasmine (*Trachelospermum jasminoides*) that climbs rustic frames of hazel branches.

30m long, with a subdividing wall across the back with a gate into a working area. The garden finishes with some large trees. Although it had a strong foundation block, the garden lacked character and atmosphere.

Because the surrounding gardens are dominated by huge plane trees, the new garden had to have enough vertical scale to register against them. I decided to keep the lawn and raised beds, but add to them. The owner likes Paris parks and wanted a calm green space as an antidote to the hustle of London streets.

I suggested that although the new design should have a formal structure, the garden could retain a country feel that was not too clinical. The terrace had plants growing between the paving, and we kept that effect and I added to it by taking out some paving and putting in roses and oregano.

The garden is now divided into three areas: the terrace, the working area at the end and the mid section with lawn that forms the main vista and axis. Each side flagstone paths give vistas to the end of the garden.

To keep the calm canvas of greens and because the garden is so structured, I felt that it did not need many flowers in summer, just a few in a deep crushed raspberry with an antique look. I used *Papaver orientale* 'Patty's Plum', an oriental poppy in a deep claret fading to dusky plum, and *Rosa* 'Viridiflora'. From the calm green of summer the planting moves into red and orange berries of holly and *Iris foetidissima*, the coppery leaves of beech and pale blue *Iris unguicularis*.

The garden now has structure and form, and a refined sense of place that suits the house and its owner. It is a calm and intensely green oasis in the middle of London studded with so few flowers that they are like jewels in the green canvas. As you walk beneath the oak trees it is hard to imagine that one of London's busiest streets hurtles by at the end of the road.

above The owner wanted the space to be predominantly green, and any flowers had to be unobtrusive and subtle. *Rosa* 'Viridiflora' is an old-fashioned rose whose green petals are tinged with red.

p149
top left The house wall has a little 1920s greenhouse that was restored and painted ochre inside to tie in with the fountain. On the terrace we added a copy of a flamboyant Regency linen umbrella lined and tasselled with red silk. Beneath it is an intimate space with an oak table and chairs for summer suppers.

top right The pots in the garden vary in size and shape but they are all made of the same material at the same pottery, which gives them a strong identity and unity.

bottom left At a sub-axis half-way down the lawn against the wall there is an arbour of lovely old beams with *Vitis coignetiae* and *Rosa* 'Gloire de Dijon' growing over it. A lantern hangs from the beams over a green semi-circular Edwardian seat backed by a box hedge. The whole area was inspired by the bench.

bottom right Opposite the arbour was an existing wall fountain that needed softening, so I limewashed it in an ochre colour.

rus in urbe

Set in a particularly spacious and green environment this garden is close to the centre of London, but the streets are wide and the houses are set back from the road giving a relaxed and less claustrophobic atmosphere than areas where terraced houses are crammed together. The spirit of the place is bohemian and less formal than in most of the capital.

The Victorian stucco house has large rooms full of paintings. The furnishings are pale with old country chairs covered in linen. Some of the rooms have stone floors and there is a modern wooden staircase. The owners love to cook and there is contemporary stainless steel in the kitchen. Everywhere there is a mix of the

traditional and the contemporary. The house has a modern extension at one side, so the merging of new and old became a starting point for the garden. The owners wanted to have traditional roots and elements of a country garden so that it felt like an established garden with a contemporary twist.

The walled plot is about 22 x 22m. When I first saw the garden it had a lawn surrounded with curved beds completely overgrown with shrubs, and suburban planting. It lacked structure and excitement. There was virtually no foundation block apart from some lime trees at the end, an elder tree and a bay tree. So I started from scratch, even replacing the terrace.

I wanted to create a circulation route that ran around the edge, with a nucleus in the middle. The owners had a wish list that included rose and vegetable gardens and herbaceous beds, and I was able to add to them by splitting the garden into various rooms around a central, formal herbaceous garden. At one side I designed a rose garden, on the other a nuttery and a potager. I made the side and end divisions the same size as the terrace, leaving a square in the middle with a central axis and vista to a fountain at the end.

I pleached the existing lime trees at the end of the garden to form a huge screen 6-8m high, which helped to make the garden feel established. From the terrace,

above The living willow arches define the sub-axis along the vegetable garden path. From the terrace you can look through a wonderful tunnel of nasturtiums to a secluded seating area at the far end of the garden.

far left The centre of the garden gives space surrounded by side gardens. Here, posts and wires for espaliered fruit form a transparent screen between the central herbaceous and vegetable gardens.

key

1   vegetable garden
2   herbaceous lawn garden
3   nuttery fountain garden
4   breakfast terrace
5   rose garden
6   main terrace

which I matched to the interior stone of the house, I created paths through the side gardens with sub-axes coming off. And because the garden can be looked down on from the house, I wanted to create a pattern on the ground. To do this I framed each corner of the central area with L-shaped yew hedges. In front of these are herbaceous beds defined with low box hedges around a central lawn. The design is rooted in classical gardens of the sixteenth and seventeenth centuries. The herbaceous beds bloom in late summer and early autumn. The main colours are burnt orange, purple and pale yellow using heleniums, Michaelmas daisies, salvias, agapanthus and monardas, mingled with many herbs.

The potager has eight oak-edged square beds with herbs and vegetables to supply the kitchen. A tunnel of living willow hoops with nasturtiums clambering over them gives a contemporary feel. Espaliered fruit trees complete this side garden. Across the lawn, in the rose garden, roses clamber over hazel domes and drape profuse pale apricot and cream flowers in June, underplanted with foxgloves (*Digitalis* 'Apricot Beauty').

A French eighteenth-century octagonal stone fountain, which the owners found, creates a focal point at the end of the garden. To help it look well

right Clambering over willow arches
nasturtiums add colour and energy
to the shady side of the garden.

established I planted four huge hazel bushes around it. Under them is a woodland planting of ferns, hellebores and foxgloves. To one side is the existing bay tree with a table and chairs beneath, and on the other is the elder tree with two seats and a bench. On the terrace is a large table for dining, surrounded by many pots.

The sense of place in this garden is so right and well-established it is hard to believe that it is only five years old. This is due mainly to the design, but other factors help. Dressing down with accessories and plants helps to give a garden a 'lived-in' look. The antique feel of the garden objects helps to give the garden history. The undercoat planting of digitalis and erigeron relaxes and settles the garden and even the snowdrops in the lawn give a country air.

The finished garden has captured many elements of a big country garden in a relatively small, town space, and is truly *rus in urbe* with an established feeling of antiquity. It is a welcoming garden whose overall sense of place is one of tranquillity and timelessness.

far left The fountain at the end of the main axis of the garden is bathed in tranquil green light cast by the surrounding hazel bushes. Beneath, a planting of ferns and hellebores intensifies the mood.

left Adding old café seats to this intimate area beyond the vegetable garden helps to give the feeling of a well-established garden.

right Not all garden objects need to be practical. Here, decoratively rusting French iron seats have become intricately entwined with the plants that surround them.

bottom On the breakfast terrace, a table by furniture maker Paul Anderson has an informal collection of chairs that relax the area for spontaneous breakfasts and lunches.

wildlife and wetlands trust garden

The Wetlands Centre, the London site of the Wildlife and Wetlands Trust, is astonishing. The 105 acres of wetland habitat is seasonal home to 130 wild bird species, many kinds of butterfly, moth and dragonfly and four species of amphibians. Its lakes, channels and ponds form a beautiful watery mosaic on the south bank of the River Thames at Barnes. Inside, it is difficult to believe that Westminster is only four miles away.

The site was originally a series of Victorian reservoirs. In its place WWT created several lakes surrounded by wetland habitat. I was one of three designers invited to design a sustainable wildlife and bio-diverse garden for a wetland site that would encourage visitors to make their own gardens wildlife friendly. With that in mind I created a natural garden that could be home to amphibians and invertebrates.

I was allocated a plot about 20m in diameter. In the centre was a curved pond with bulrushes and marginal plants and the rest was boggy, treeless scrub. I wanted the garden to stem from the water and felt that it should have structure and a loose formality but with the wildness of nature. Above all, I wanted the garden to be as natural as possible and to echo to the spiritual sites of antiquity, when water was worshipped.

One of my inspirations was Flag Fen near Peterborough, an area highly populated in the Bronze Age with a rich source of food and reeds for building shelter. Flag Fen once had forests of silver birches so I decided to plant many of them to help give the garden an established, ancient feel.

right From the turf seat at the centre of the garden concentric circles of log walls radiate like ripples in water. They form an energetic and unusual backbone and a haven for wildlife.

left We preserved the original planting at the water's edge and allowed it to meld sympathetically with the log walls.

above To give the backbone antiquity the silver birches are planted to look as if they have colonized an ancient site naturally.

I left the pond just as it was and decided against flowing water or adding artificial fountains. My inspiration for the overall design was the concentric, widening ripples that a pebble makes when thrown into water. I began by drawing these on the master plan, making them radiate from the pond.

My next problem was how to make these concentric ripples on the site. I wanted all the materials in the garden to be sustainable, so I used split oak logs and piled them into curving and undulating walls about 1m high to represent the ripples. The circles are broken in places: some log walls just dip into the pond and stop,

some form a bridge across the water. The logs are stacked in the same way as a woodpile, and form excellent habitats for many different kinds of creatures.

To add to the ancient and spiritual atmosphere, the undulating walls needed to be softened. Along the top of some I laid wild-flower turf to give them the look of ancient earthworks. Once in place, the log-wall circles had a strong feeling of antiquity and the spirituality of stone circles, with echoes of pagan civilizations.

The site is managed in the spirit of the wilderness, just to keep the water clear. It is now home to newts, frogs, toads, mice and many insects. The garden will not stay the same; as the oak logs rot different insects and fungi will colonize it, but being oak it will last at least 20 years. In 50 years there will still be hummocks, and the ring formation will be like an ancient earthwork.

The garden's spiritual quality is intense. When visitors stand in the centre of the inner circle many find the atmosphere quite powerful. I think this is partly because the log-wall circles have a similar effect to ancient stone circles and, of course, because of the beauty of the site. There is a compelling air of antiquity and enigma about the garden that is enhanced by the veil of plants. They form a green mist over the site and add to its mystical quality.

left above and below I wanted the planting to be wild and natural, and as veil-like as possible. I used great burnet (*Sanguisorba officinalis*), foxgloves, white rosebay, Euphorbia polychroma, camassia and dropwort. Grasses included *Molinia caerulea arundinacea* 'Karl Foerster' and tufted hair grass (*Deschampsia caespitosa*), with clumps of sculptural reeds at the edge of the pond. The existing water and marginal plants were left as they were.

my fenland garden

The first time I saw my Lincolnshire house was on a cold, sunny March day. As I drove across from Suffolk the countryside got flatter and flatter and appeared isolated and very frontier like. There were virtually no trees or hedgerows, just unending open space and voluminous skies. There was an air of excitement and challenge about the environment, but at the same time I felt rather vulnerable in the vast, open landscape.

The plot surrounding the house was mostly field overgrown with brambles, and in some parts the plough line of the surrounding farmland came right up to the house. It is about five acres in total, but about three acres are orchard and grazing. The only foundation block was a huge, ancient yew tree centred on the front of the house, and parts of the garden walls. What garden existed was haphazardly dotted with silver birch trees, elders and rusting corrugated iron sheds. There was a tired herbaceous garden in front of the house.

The site is slightly raised above the surrounding Fenland which makes it dry enough for a house, and there has been some sort of settlement here since Roman times and probably before that too. The earliest part of the present house goes back to about 1520 and the rest is seventeenth century. The soft, red brick building with its big windows and the quality of light that they filter feels as Dutch as the landscape. The house is furnished in William and Mary style and the prevailing atmosphere is one of serenity and of time gently standing still.

The sense of place is not just about the house though: it seems to permeate through the soil because the site is so ancient. Instinctively I felt that the house and garden should hold hands and make an effortless link. I also wanted to create an environment of safety and protection around the house that it did not have when I first saw it.

I had the luxury of time and spent the first two years observing the plot to see what came up. I got the feel of what was there, and began to plan what to keep and to formulate my new design. The surrounding landscape had a profound influence on the making of the garden. It did not take long to discover that the wind was the deciding factor. Even on the hottest day it swept straight in from the North Sea 10 miles away so creating shelter was essential.

I loved the ancient yew, so that had to stay. And I decided to keep the old apple trees and the orchard, but I needed to get a good blank canvas to work on so the silver birches and the sheds had to go. I had bonfire after bonfire to clear the scrub and elders. Then I began work on the backbone. The starting point of the garden was the magnificent yew, which I cut back to a topiary column so that the garden and view could be seen from the house. The main axis of the garden runs through the centre of the yew, and I edged it with a cloud of lavender that spills on to the central path. Other axes and divisions for new garden rooms went in later.

The viciousness of the wind made shelter a priority, so I put in the lime trees for the pleached lime walk and planted windbreak hedges as soon as I could.

That same year I built the walls around the kitchen garden, and repaired the potting shed and other outbuildings that run along one side. The walls gave the kitchen garden a microclimate that was quite different from the rest of the cold, exposed site and once they were in place I could grow the plants I wanted.

right Along the main axis of the garden is the 300-year-old yew. Part of the foundation block, this magnificent tree matches the boldness of the house and connects the garden to its ancient site.

key

1 mount
2 orchard
3 wilderness garden
4 winter knot garden
5 rose garden
6 physic garden
7 pleached lime garden
8 herbaceous garden
9 lawn parterre
10 kitchen garden

above When I open the oak door in the wall and step into the garden I have an overwhelming sense that I have come into an oasis in an unrelenting and rather forbidding landscape of prairie and sky.

left A row of formal topiaried eleagnus marks the boundary of the terrace. They have an excellent sense of scale with the house and set off the deep crimson *Cirsium rivulare* 'Atropurpureum', allowing their vibrancy to shine.

This success crystallized the rest of the garden plan. I created a design based on sheltered garden rooms surrounded by a backbone of protective hedges. Each room flows to the next via axes, sub-axes and vistas.

The walled herbaceous garden around the yew tree in front of the house leads to the cool, green, pleached lime walk, which opens on to a physic garden through a sculptural gap in the hedge. A change of level between two pavilions draws one into the serpentine rose garden, which in turn leads into the sheltered knot garden. The boundary hedge also encloses an orchard with a mount, and a wilderness garden planted with aconites and snowdrops. Along the axes there are 'doorways', or sculptural gaps, cut in the hedge to give tantalizing views of the countryside beyond and to link the garden back to the landscape.

In its planting and style the garden reflects the evolution and history of gardening, but it looks to the future too – it is timeless. It refers back to the things I love in gardening history, but adds a contemporary twist. The garden is about all the passions that influence me from history, design, architecture and nature and the ways it can be manipulated.

The physic garden has square beds like those of mediaeval physic gardens. Its strength is in the simplicity of the planting that refers to the past. In the oak-edged beds beneath holm oak (*Quercus ilex*) I used *Iris* 'Florentina' because the Romans used to

right In the herbaceous garden the energy of strong purples, reds and oranges such as *Centranthus ruber*, *Salvia verticillata* 'Purple Rain', *Cirsium rivulare* 'Atropurpureum', and various monardas, matches the power of the surrounding landscape.

make a perfume from its roots. At the end of the physic garden, in an embracing hedge, is a curved stone bench that is a perfect place for a drink on a summer evening. The pleached lime walk echoes those of the Tudor period, but it also has a contemporary feel because it is minimalist with clean, crisp lines.

The whole garden has a profound sense of place and each garden room has its own mood. The rose garden has an energized upbeat feel strengthened by the curving serpentine hedges and the pink, blue-purple and bronze planting. The physic garden is more tranquil and contemplative centred on a stone fountain that gently drips into a pool. The herbaceous garden has plenty of zing, while the lime walk is all calm green.

The garden's atmosphere is now serene – it is a safe haven with order, formality and, in contrast with beyond the boundary, control of nature. It is an oasis for wildlife as well as people: now the hedges and trees have grown there are countless birds, bees and butterflies where once there were none. With time the garden's structure is becoming more layered and the sense of place changes in a slow dance as the garden matures.

left Although it draws on a traditional Elizabethan pattern the design of the knot garden is executed in a contemporary style by using solid platforms of beech instead of box. It is a well-protected site and even in January I can take a cup of coffee out and sit on the seat against the warm wall of the house.

below The kitchen garden probably has the strongest atmosphere of the whole garden and is intensely protective and meditative. The walls have made such a difference to its shelter that even experienced Fenland gardeners are astonished at what I manage to grow in it. And we can grow crops throughout the year.

Many people have helped to formulate my ideas over the years and to all those who helped me along the garden path I give thanks, especially Peter Hone who taught me so much when I worked for him at Clifton Little Venice, and my mother and brothers Uwe, Michael and Lars who never failed to give me encouragement.

At work, Richard Miers and Julia Aschenbach have held the fort with immense patience while I have worked on the book.

I would also like to thank my clients for their faith in allowing me to try out my ideas in their gardens, which are featured in the Case Studies, especially David and Eve Abbott, Lyn and Albert Fuss, June and Jon Summerill and The Wildlife and Wetlands Trust.

Sue Seddon has been a tower of strength in guiding me through a steep learning curve and has so sympathetically and eloquently put into words my ideas and feelings.

Finally, I could never have managed without the support of William Collinson who took many of the beautiful photographs in this book and read the manuscript with honesty.

Arne Maynard

Rosie Atkins, Editor of *Gardens Illustrated*, has a gift for bringing people together. She thought we would work well as a team and introduced us. We are extremely grateful to her for setting us on the path to a hugely enjoyable collaboration and for all her support.

Our thanks too to the many friends who have listened, encouraged and supported us throughout the project.

We are also very grateful to Mel Watson for her infinite patience and expertize in finding so many magnificent photographs and to Lucy Holmes, who brought words and pictures together in such a superb design.

Arne's enthusiasm, trust and loyalty have been a delight. Writing with him has been a great pleasure and a lot of fun, especially when we worked at his home in Lincolnshire, where Hazel the dog stood guard over every discarded sheet of paper and the hospitality and company are so warm and welcoming.

Sue Seddon

2 Dennis Gilbert/View/Architect: Edward Cullinan; 5 Marcus Harpur/The Garden in an Orchard, Norfolk/Sculptor Jonathan Keep; 6 S & O Mathews; 8–9 Andrea Jones/The Garden Picture Library; 10–11 Stephen Robson; 13 Country Life Magazine/Alex Ramsay; 14 Henk Dijkman/Designer: Henk Weijers; 15 above Deidi von Schaewen; 15 below Andrew Lawson; 16 Jerry Harpur/Coton Manor, Northants; 17 above Clay Perry/Artist: Andy Goldsworthy, Grizedale Forest Park, Cumbria; 17 below The National Trust Photo Library/Nick Meers/Snowshill Manor Glos; 18 above Andrew Lawson/The Garden House, Devon; 18 centre Deidi von Schaewen/Designer: Nicole de Vesian; 18 below Andrew Lawson/Artist: Ian Hamilton Finlay; 19 David Glomb/Architect: Richard Neutra (Marmol and Radziner); 20 Jerry Harpur/Designer: Isabelle C. Greene, CA, USA; 21 above Jerry Harpur/King Henry's Hunting Lodge; 21 below Deidi von Schaewen/Rosenberg, NY; 22 Henk Dijkman; 23 Jerry Harpur/Designer: Galen Lee, New York; 25 above left and below right Andrew Lawson; 25 above right and below left Ian Smith/Acres Wild Garden Design; 26–27 Deidi von Schaewen/Prieuré d'Orsan, France; 29 Vivian Russell; 30 above Andrew Lawson/Hatfield House, Herts; 30 centre National Trust Photo Library/Montacute, Somerset; 30 below Edifice/Dunnell; 31 Derek St Romaine/Weald and Downland Museum; 32 The Colonial Williamsburg Foundation; 32–33 National Trust Photo Library/Stephen Robson/Ham House, Surrey; 34 National Trust Photo Library/Ian Shaw/Wightwick Manor, West Midlands; 35 National Trust Photo Library/Stephen Robson/ Packwood House, Warks; 36 Edifice/Lewis; 37 Jerry Harpur/Designer:

Arthur Ericksson, Vancouver; 39 Marion Brenner/Bowes House, Sonoma, USA/Garden Designer: Roger Warner; 41 above Fritz von der Schulenburg/The Interior Archive/Designer: Adelheid von der Schulenburg; 41 below National Trust Photo Library/Andrea Jones/The Vyne, Hampshire; 42 above Marijke Heuff/Beckley Park; 42 below left Simon Upton/ The Interior Archive/Artist: Celia Lyttleton; 42 below right Clay Perry/The Garden Picture Library; 43 National Trust Photo Library/Andreas von Einsiedel/Moseley Old Hall, Staffs; 44 Paul Ryan/International Interiors/Designers: J. Saladino/S.Casdin; 44–45 The Colonial Williamsburg Foundation; 46 Vivien Russell/Gardens Illustrated; 49 Camera Press/Gert von Bassewitz/Hauser Magazine; 50 Jerry Harpur/Benington Lordship, Herts; 51 Jerry Harpur/Designer: Isabelle C. Greene, CA, USA; 53 Sunniva Harte/Folkington Place, Sussex; 54 left Edifice/Ryle-Hodges; 54 right Marijke Heuff; 55 National Trust Photo Library/Stephen Robson/Nymans Garden, West Sussex; 56–57 Vivian Russell; 59 Andrew Lawson/Designer: Ivan Hicks; 61 above left Juliette Wade; 61 centre left Marijke Heuff/Mr & Mrs van Vyve, Belgium; 61 below left Gary Rogers; 61 right Anne Hyde 62 Mayer/Le Scanff/The Garden Picture Library/Domaine de Rioucougourde, France; 63 J C Mayer – G Le Scanff/Le Baque (47) France; 64 Piet Oudolf; 65 Deidi von Schaewen/L. Williams, France; 66–67 John Glover/Designer: Alex Champion, California; 69 Jerry Harpur/ Shore Hall, Essex; 70 above Brigitte Thomas/The Garden Picture Library/Levens Hall, Cumbria; 70 below Richard Felber; 71 National Trust Photo Library/Stephen Robson/Lytes Cary Manor, Somerset; 73 above Jerry Harpur/Hatfield House, Herts; 73 below Jerry

Harpur/Manor House, Bledlow, Bucks; 74 above Marianne Majerus/Heale House, Wilts; 74 below William Collinson; 76 J C Mayer – G Le Scanff/Landscape Designer: Kathryn Gustafson, Les Jardins de l'imaginaire, (24) Terrasson, France; 78 Crown Copyright N.M.R.; 80 Juliette Wade/Rofford Manor, Oxon, NGS; 81 Christopher Simon Sykes/The Interior Archive/Nancy McCabe/Private Landscapes; 82 Marijke Heuff/Gourdon, France; 83 above Jerry Harpur/Hatfield House, Herts; 83 below Philippe Bonduel; 84 Richard Felber; 84–85 Jerry Harpur/Designer: Davis Dalbok, San Francisco, USA; 86 above Roger Foley/Colonial Williamsburg, USA; 86 below Marijke Heuff/Rosendal/Designer: Simon Irvine; 88–89 John Glover/The Garden Picture Library; 91 Mayer/Le Scanff/The Garden Picture Library; 92–93 John Glover/The Garden Picture Library; 94 above left Jerry Harpur/Shore Hall, Essex; 94 above right Marijke Heuff/La Berquerie, Designer: Mark Brown; 94 below Jerry Harpur/Designer: Arabella Lennox-Boyd; 95 above Sunniva Harte/The Garden Picture Library; 95 below John Glover/The Garden Picture Library/RHS Wisley; 96–97 Christi Carter/The Garden Picture Library; 98 above left Ron Evans/The Garden Picture Library; 98 above right Andrew Lawson/Sticky Wicket, Dorset; 98 below Clay Perry/The Garden Picture Library; 99 above Sunniva Harte/The Garden Picture Library; 99 below left Jacqui Hurst/The Garden Picture Library; 99 below right Modeste Herwig/Ton Ter Linden; 100–101 Didier Willery/The Garden Picture Library; 102 David Cavagnaro/The Garden Picture Library; 103 above left Ron Evans/The Garden Picture Library; 103 above right Mayer/Le Scanff/The Garden Picture Library; 103 below John Glover/The Garden Picture Library;

104 William Collinson; 107 Jerry Harpur/Villa Cetinale, Italy; 108 above Sunniva Harte/Great Dixter, East Sussex; 108 below Hugh Palmer/Villa Pisani, Italy; 109 National Trust Photo Library/Neil Campbell-Sharp/Castle Drogo, Devon; 110 Kate Gadsby/Wyken Hall, Suffolk; 111 William Collinson; 112 above Richard Felber; 112 below Piet Oudolf; 113 Jerry Harpur/Designer: Keeyla Meadows, San Francisco, USA; 114 above Marianne Majerus/Fondation Maeght, St Paul-de-Vence, France; 114 below Marijke Heuff/Mr & Mrs van Vyve, Belgium; 115 National Trust Photo Library/Neil Campbell-Sharp/Montacute, Somerset; 116–117 Colin Varndell/Bruce Coleman; 119 Edifice/Darley; 120 Andrew Lawson/Magdalen College, Oxford; 121–122 Bob Gibbons/Woodfall Wild Images Ltd; 123 Hans Reinhard/Bruce Coleman; 124 Sunniva Harte/Great Dixter, East Sussex; 125 above left Jerry Harpur/Rousham, Oxon; 125 above right Yann Monel/Chateau de Saint-Just, France; 125 below Clay Perry/Artist: Richard Harris, Grizedale Forest Park, Cumbria; 126 J S Sira/The Garden Picture Library; 127 above John Heseltine/Bruce Coleman; 127 below J C Mayer – G Le Scanff/Domaine de Saint Jean de Beauregard (91), France; 129 above left The Art Archive; 129 above right National Trust Photo Library/John Hammond/Montacute House, Somerset; 129 below left The National Gallery; 129 below right Jerry Harpur/Heale House, Wilts; 130 William Collinson/RHS Chelsea 2000/Designers: Arne Maynard & Piet Oudolf; 131 Rebecca Lloyd/RHS Chelsea 2000/Designers: Arne Maynard & Piet Oudolf; 132–134 William Collinson; 137–143 Andrew Lawson; 144–149 William Collinson; 150–155 Andrew Lawson; 156–171 William Collinson.